West Academic Publishing's Law School Advisory Board

a short & happy guide to Employment Law

Ann C. Juliano
Professor of Law
Villanova University
Charles Widger School of Law

A SHORT & HAPPY GUIDE® SERIES

WEST ACADEMIC

860 Blue Gentian Road, Suite 350
Eagan, MN 55121
1-877-888-1330

Published in the United States of America

ISBN: 978-1-63659-512-2

Again and always, for Matt and the Women of Winding Way.

Acknowledgments

Thank you to all the workers at gyms and hair salons and offices I've quizzed over the years about their jobs ("Did you sign a noncompete? Would you say you're an employee?") and all the employers who have chatted with me about the issues they face in their workforce.

Thank you to West Academic for entrusting me with another Short and Happy Guide and for the patience in awaiting its completion. To the crew of students who read chapters and offered their helpful insights and suggestions, my gratitude to Catie Barry ('24), Tony Cassetta ('24), Grace Gelone ('24), Meggie McCarthy-White ('24), Caity Rogowski ('24), David Tilli ('25), and especially Domenica Tomasetti ('23).

There aren't enough smoothies in the world to thank Lauren Getman ('25) for her incredible help in bringing this project to conclusion.

Thanks again to Jennifer O'Hare for being the listening ear and checker of formats.

Table of Contents

A Short & Happy Guide to Employment Law

CHAPTER 1

Employment Law

We all work (well, most of us work; maybe you have a trust fund). That's the great thing about learning Employment Law. For many of the topics discussed in this book, you have already thought about them. Are they allowed to ask me that in an interview? How much will I get paid? What benefits do I get? Is this workplace safe? What if I get hurt at work? What happens if I get fired? Some of you have been in charge of hiring so you know the other side of these questions: how can I make sure someone is the right employee for us? Can I fire this person? Can I tell them what to wear or what posters they can have in their cubicle? And we haven't even discussed the most important question for workers—are you an employee or an independent contractor?

Our society tries to accomplish many things through our employment laws. It's a never-ending balancing act between allowing employers to manage their business as they wish and providing protection for societal values. The anti-discrimination laws limit the employer's ability to hire (or fire). Contract and tort law also restrict that ability. We require the employer to take action to protect worker safety and to provide for workers when they are injured due to the job. Employer provided health care is a seemingly never-ending battle. It may appear that the law expects too much of employers or it may seem that not enough is provided for workers, depending of course on your personal views.

Employment law truly is about resolving this conflict between employers and workers. What must the employer do? What may the employer do? What may the workers do? This balance of interests is constantly shifting and evolving. Employment law always has to respond to new developments. Think of all the employment issues which arose during the COVID-19 pandemic or the still evolving issues surrounding the legalization of cannabis. We can only imagine what will come next!

Understanding the rights of workers and the rights and obligations of employers involves an overlapping system of federal, state, and local laws. If the workplace is a public employer, the U.S. Constitution is involved as well. It's a lot, people. Although there are many federal employment laws, much about these issues are resolved by state law. This book cannot provide a comprehensive overview as to how all of these issues are resolved in every state or it would be need to be named "The Long & Overwhelming Guide to Employment Law." Another important source of rights and duties in the workplace are collective bargaining agreements. This Short & Happy guide does not address the area of collective action in the workplace but rather focuses on the rights and duties of employers and individual workers.

The starting place for employment is the doctrine known as "employment at will." The (almost cliché) description of employment at will is that an employer may fire an employee for a good reason, a bad reason, or no reason at all (just not a prohibited reason). Conversely, an employee may quit for a good reason, a bad reason, or no reason. This doctrine, in American law, is attributed to a fellow named Horace Wood. In a treatise written in the late 1800s, old Horace declared: "[w]ith us the rule is inflexible, that a general or indefinite hiring is prima facie a hiring at will, and if the servant seeks to make it out a yearly hiring, the burden is upon him to establish it by proof."[1] There is some question as to whether Horace accurately reported the state of the law at the time. Regardless, this statement quickly became the law of the land.

Since that writing, there are now numerous restrictions on the employer's ability to fire workers. Any time an employer must have "cause" to fire is a restriction on employment at will. An employment contract may contain restrictions. The civil service system and the tenure system have restrictions on the employer's ability to fire workers on a whim. Finally, some employee handbooks or manuals limit the reasons why a worker may be terminated.

Now, you may have noticed that this introduction uses the term "worker" instead of employee. That is because the very first question we must ask in the Employment Law setting is whether the worker is an employee or an independent contractor. So many of the rights that flow from the statutes apply only to those workers who are deemed to be an "employee." (That's why this topic is covered in the very next chapter.)

Chapter Three discusses becoming an employee. Think back to when you were hired for a job. The employer has to make sure that you are eligible to work in the United States and that their methods of hiring (job posting, interviews, screenings) are legal. Chapter Four covers the federal anti-discrimination laws, another important source of rights for employees. This chapter is a summary of a very big topic.[2] Then we'll turn to the question of wages and hours for the all important question for workers—how much am I getting paid and how many hours do I have to work? Chapter Six discusses employer provided healthcare.

---

1 Horace Wood, A Treatise on the Law of Master & Servant 272 (1877).

2 For a fuller discussion of this area, go grab a copy of The Short & Happy Guide to Employment Discrimination!

Then we turn to other areas of rights and protections for workers. Chapter Seven covers occupational safety and the system of worker's compensation when those safety measures fail. Chapter Eight covers the source of many conflicts between employers and workers—what is collectively known as employee liberty. Questions such as speech and dress and privacy matters are covered in this chapter.

Chapter Nine, Ten, and Eleven cover the end of the employment relationship. Chapter Nine sets forth the restrictions on the employer's ability to terminate employment from statutory restrictions to constitutional law to contract and tort law. Chapter Ten discusses the obligations of employees during and after employment. Non-compete agreements (another ever evolving issue) and trade secrets fall on the employee side of the obligations. Chapter Eleven turns to the post-employment obligations of employers, including unemployment insurance. Finally, Chapter Eleven discusses employer obligations for retirement, including pensions and the federal statutory requirements. This book ends with a brief overview of arbitration

By the end of this book, you will have an overview of ALL of the issues that employers and workers face in the workplace. You'll be ready to dive into the details for whatever state and topic is before you. You'll be happy and you'll be informed. Ready? Let's go!

CHAPTER 2

Defining Employee and Employer

It may seem like a simple question to determine when someone is an "employee". However, not everyone who works for someone else is considered an employee. Consider your own jobs: that stint during the summer at the ice cream parlor? You were an employee. Your summer associate position? Employee. Tutoring for a test prep company? Hmmm, are you an employee of the test prep company, or the parents who paid you? Or maybe you are an independent contractor? What about a tech consultant to a company working on commission? Determining a worker's classification is important because employees are entitled to several protections and benefits that do not extend to independent contractors.

Lots has been written about today's "gig" economy—people working different tasks for different employers, without full-time employment at any one workplace. The gig economy has created further uncertainty in the area of who counts as an employee. Perhaps most well-known are issues surrounding ride-share companies like Uber and Lyft.[1] The same issues apply to people who

[1] Several court decisions have addressed the question as to whether Uber drivers are "employees." For example, here are a few cases where the court discusses

work for companies such as Instacart or Door Dash. One student in my class, Lyndsey, told the class that she worked for a dog walking company as a gig worker, taking jobs whenever she had time. Suppose Lyndsey fell when the dog yanked on the leash—would she be entitled to worker's compensation? Imagine if Lyndsey had a vacation coming up and she decided to work 50 hours over one week (a week during which she did not have classes, obviously). Would she be entitled to overtime pay?

These protections and many others all turn on whether the worker can be classified as an employee. Employee protections include wage and hour laws,[2] worker's compensation, the anti-discrimination statutes, the Family and Medical Leave Act ("FMLA"), unemployment compensation, workplace safety, and pension protections. Whether a worker qualifies for these protections depends on their status as an employee. So let's leap into these definitions.

A. Who Counts as an Employee?

Typically, the question is whether a worker is an employee or an independent contractor. Employment law statutes do, on occasion, provide definitions, but these definitions are incredibly unhelpful. For example, Title VII (an anti-discrimination statute) defines employee as "any individual employed by an employer." Seriously. The Fair Labor Standards Act ("FLSA") uses the same definition but further defines "employ" as "to suffer or permit to work." Charming. Faced with such circular reasoning, courts have developed a series of tests to determine a worker's status. Not to give away any spoilers, but . . . these tests overlap.

---

the issue: Tyler v. Uber Technologies, Inc., 487 F. Supp.3d 27 (D.D.C. 2020); Narayanasamy v. Issa, 435 F.Supp.3d 388 (D.R.I. 2020); O'Connor v. Uber Technologies, Inc., 82 F.Supp.3d 1133 (N.D. Cal. 2015).

[2] The Fair Labor Standards Act, 29 U.S.C. § 203, is the federal law which sets minimum wage and when overtime must be paid (among other things).

1. Control Test: "You're not the boss of me!"

The first test is known as the **control test** and it arose out of respondeat superior cases (where a party is injured by a worker and wants to sue the employer in order to recover greater damages). Relying on agency law,[3] courts turned to the "master-servant" relationship (yes, it's actually called that). This test is also referred to as the common law test. Under the control test, there is no shorthand formula for determining who is an "employee," and so multiple factors must be assessed and weighed when reviewing an employment relationship. There are a few different versions of this multi-factor test floating around but the focus remains on the ability of one party to control the other party. In other words, the court considers not just what the job is, but to what extent the business controls how to do the job. Therefore, one way to view the "control" is to examine the level and amount of supervision the employer has over the worker.

In the leading Supreme Court case on this question, *Nationwide Mutual Insurance Co. v. Darden*, a case determining the meaning of "employee" under the Employee Retirement Income Security Act ("ERISA"), the Court set forth several factors to review in applying the control test:

- the skill required
- who provided the tools necessary to complete the job
- the location of the work
- the duration of the relationship
- whether the hiring party can assign additional tasks to the worker

[3] If you haven't heard of the term "agency law," it simply means the common law that governs the relationship between a principal and an agent.

- whether the hiring party can determine the hours of the worker
- if the work is part of the regular business of the hiring party
- the provision of employee benefits.[4]

Courts have differed over the importance of each of these factors, but the focus remains on the central question of control of one party over the other. In addition to ERISA, this test has been applied to the National Labor Relations Act ("NLRA") and the Federal Unemployment Tax Act ("FUTA").

2. *Economic Realities Test: "You can take this job and. . ."*

Under the **economic realities test**, which grew out of a case under the NLRA, courts look to see if (1) the worker is economically dependent on the employer or (2) the worker is not reliant on one employer for all his hours and tasks. The test uses a totality of the circumstances approach, which is a more flexible approach than the multi-factor control test. In essence, the fundamental question is: may the worker set out on her own hours and tasks or must she rely on the employer?

In shocking news to no law student ever, to help answer this fundamental question, courts have developed more factors for the economic realities test:

- the degree of the putative employer's right to control the manner in which the work is to be performed;
- the worker's opportunity for profit or loss;

---

[4] Nationwide Mutual Insurance Co. v. Darden, 503 U.S. 318, 323 (1992).

- who purchased the necessary equipment;
- whether special skill is involved;
- the degree of permanence of the working relationship; and,
- whether the service rendered is an integral part of the business.[5]

I'm sure that you, a careful reader, have noticed that many of the factors from the control test and the economic realities test overlap. The main difference in the tests is the weight placed on the first factor listed above, sometimes known as the "control factor." As a "totality of the circumstances" test, the economic realities test is more flexible and places less importance on the control factor. This test is applied to questions under the FLSA, the Occupational Safety and Health Act ("OSHA"), and federal anti-discrimination statutes.

3. *Hybrid Test: Just smush them all together*

Several federal courts have employed (get it?) a test which combines elements of the control test and the economic realities test. Often this is in the context of the anti-discrimination statutes. Under the **hybrid test**, courts consider all the economic realities test's factors, but places great emphasis on the employer's right to control the work.

4. *ABC Test: "But I am an employee"*

Attempting to bring more certainty to the issue, some states have enacted statutes to broaden the definition of employee.[6]

---

[5] Donovan v. DialAmerica MKTG., Inc., 757 F.2d 1376 (3d Cir. 1985).

[6] *See* California Labor Code § 2750.3 and Massachusetts Gen. Laws Ch. 149, § 149B(a) for example.

Known as the **ABC test**, these statutes presume workers qualify as employees[7] unless the business shows each of the following:

1. The business is unable to control or direct what the worker does, either by contract or in actual practice;
2. The worker performs tasks outside of the entity's usual business; and
3. The worker is engaged in an independently established trade.

B. Who Does *Not* Count as an Employee?

Individual statutes include exclusions from the definition of "employee". Some examples include prisoners, students, trainees, domestic workers, and agricultural workers. Volunteers are generally not considered employees. However, some state laws include volunteers in the protections against workplace harassment. I know what you are thinking. "What about my unpaid legal externship???" Rest assured, this issue is addressed in Chapter 5. For now, let's consider two of the more ambiguous categories of workers: children and undocumented workers.

1. Children

Under the FLSA, children aged 14 and 15 are allowed to work in variety of non-manufacturing and non-hazardous jobs under specified circumstances (not during school hours). Children aged 16 and 17 are allowed to work for unlimited hours in any occupation unless the work is deemed hazardous. For the most part, children under 14 years of age may not legally work and therefore are not considered to be employees. However, there are exceptions for children under 14, dependent on the business. For example, these

[7] A number of professions are excepted from the statute (such as attorneys and physicians).

children may perform nonhazardous work such as working in a family business, delivering newspapers, or performing in dramatic productions. There is a different set of standards for work in agricultural occupations, allowing children even younger to work. As of this writing, a number of states have passed legislation to reduce the restrictions on child labor, including increasing the number of hours children may work and in the type of industries in which they may work.

Despite these prohibitions, courts have found children to be employees in specific cases. In cases where a child is carrying out a task and is injured, courts have been called upon to determine the child's employment status using the tests set forth above. In many of these cases, the court does not place a great deal of emphasis on the fact that the child cannot legally perform the work. Keep in mind that if the child is determined to be an employee, the child has access to worker's compensation. If the injured child is found to be an employee, they must rely on worker's compensation and is unable to sue for tort damages. Because tort damages usually far exceed worker's compensation pay-outs, employers often seek to have child workers found to be "employees."

2. Undocumented Workers

Federal immigration statutes prohibit undocumented workers from working in the United States.[8] However, as we know, there are many undocumented workers. When these workers suffer violations of employment laws, the question arises as to whether or not they may recover any remedies. The Supreme Court held in *Hoffman Plastics v. NLRB*[9] that an undocumented worker who was fired for union activity (a violation of the NLRA) could not receive the pay he

[8] *See* Chapter 4 for a discussion of the Immigration Reform and Control Act of 1986 ("IRCA").

[9] 535 U.S. 137 (2002)

lost due to the unlawful termination. So, although the worker engaged in protected activity under the NLRA, his remedies were limited. This holding has not been extended to other federal statutes, such as Title VII or the FLSA. For claims under workers' compensation programs, the ability to recover damages is dependent upon state law, with some states prohibiting undocumented workers from recovering and others allowing recovery.

C. Who Counts as an Employer?

For some statutes, a business' status as an "employer" is dependent on the number of employees it has. The anti-discrimination statutes, for example, require a minimum of 15 employees[10] or 20 employees.[11] The Family and Medical Leave Act ("FMLA") applies to businesses with 50 employees. Other statutes, such as FLSA, define employer as "any person acting directly or indirectly in the interest of an employer in relation to an employee."

The tricky questions for the definition of employer revolve around two issues: high level managers and joint employers. For example, is a partner in a law firm an employee or an employer? Remember that the anti-discrimination statutes have a threshold for the number of employees before the statute applies. Thus, for small employers, determining whether one or two people are considered employees can be the difference in coverage (and therefore liability) under federal statutes. When the Supreme Court considered this issue, it relied on Equal Employment Opportunity Commission (EEOC) guidelines and noted the focus on "control" in

---

[10] Title VII and the Americans with Disabilities Act ("ADA").

[11] Age Discrimination in Employment Act ("ADEA").

the relationship—sounds familiar, right? The Court rejected a focus on job titles and set forth yet ANOTHER multi-factor test.[12]

The second issue of joint employers can arise in a number of ways. First, imagine Fred works for Company A and Company A sends Fred to work for Company B. Company B then fails to pay Fred overtime wages. Which company is Fred's employer for purposes of recovering the wages? Courts look to the same factors as the control test for employees. This is a very fact specific test, which can result in both companies being found to be responsible as joint employers. If, however, Company A is controlling Fred's hours, along with where and when he works, then Company A is Fred's sole employer.

The same issue is present for parent-subsidiary structures and sister companies. Again, courts will examine the interdependence of the subsidiary with the parent company. Is the subsidiary truly independent of the parent company? If so, the subsidiary will be the sole employer. If not, it may be considered a joint employer.

For example, consider farm operators. Farms frequently use a contractor to hire and supervise the farm workers. Often, courts have found the farm operators and the labor contractors to be joint employers, dependent on factors such as housing, equipment, supervision.

> **IN SUMMARY:** Statutes have specific definitions of employee and employer. Often, the definition of employee is circular and doesn't really help provide an answer. To decide the question, courts have created two tests: the control test and the economic realities test.

---

[12] Clackamas Gastroenterology Associates v. Wells, 538 U.S. 440, 450 (2003). The six factors are: 1) whether the organization can hire or fire the individual or set the rules and regulations of the individual's work; 2) whether and to what extent the organization supervises the individual's work; 3) whether the individual reports to someone higher in the organization; 4) whether and to what extent, the individual is able to influence the organization; 5) whether the parties intended the individual to be an employee; and, 6) whether the individual shares in the profits, losses, and liabilities of the organization.

And then other courts smushed those tests together in a hybrid test. Some states have enacted legislation to try and provide some clarity by presuming all workers are employees unless the business is able to meet the ABC test. As for employers, definitions may be based on the number of employees at the business. Further, the definition of joint employers and how to differentiate between high level managers and employees are key to determining whether a statute applies to a business.

CHAPTER 3

Becoming an Employee

Whether hired as an at-will employee[1] or under a contract, every employee must actually become an employee. That is, you have to be hired—you can't just show up on your own, start working, and expect to be paid. The hiring process can be quite formal with multiple applications, interviews, and even tests. Or it could be quite informal. For example, perhaps in high school your friend mentioned that the ice cream parlor needed additional help. The following day you strolled in, told the boss you were there for a job, and the next thing, you had a uniform! Regardless of the method of hiring, each step comes with potential legal pitfalls.

A. The Labor Pool

Before applications are submitted, interviews are conducted, and background checks are run, employers and potential employees have a couple considerations. First, employers must determine who is eligible for their job opening. Additionally, potential employees need to learn about the job opportunity. These potential employees

---

[1] Recall from Chapter 1 that "at-will" employment means the employment may be ended at any time, by either the employer or the employee, for any reason as long as it isn't an unlawful reason.

are called the "labor pool" and represent workers that are eligible to be hired by the employer.

1. Who May Be Hired

At the beginning of the hiring process, an employer must consider whether a worker has legal authorization to work in the United States. Although sometimes the paperwork for this step doesn't occur until after a job offer, it is a threshold question of eligibility that must be met. Federal immigration statutes prohibit employers from hiring individuals who are not authorized to work in the United States. In particular, the Immigration Reform and Control Act ("IRCA") applies to all employers and requires employers to verify that workers are authorized to work in the United States. To do so, employers must ask each employee for documentation that show the individual is authorized to work. Interestingly, the employer does not have to verify the authenticity of those documents. If the employer fails to comply, it could face civil penalties. If the employer engages in a pattern of violations, there could be criminal fines and imprisonment. Such penalties could incentivize an employer to refuse to hire workers of certain nationalities on the belief that such workers are undocumented. To combat this, IRCA also forbids discrimination on the basis of national origin with similar penalties for violations of that provision.

To further complicate how IRCA governs employers, state laws may also come into play. Arizona decided that the federal government wasn't doing enough to curb unlawful immigration and enacted legislation that allowed the state to suspend or revoke the business licenses of companies that hired undocumented workers.[2] The Supreme Court ultimately upheld the Arizona law and found that the law didn't interfere with the federal immigration system.

---

[2] *See* Legal Arizona Workers Act. Florida recently adopted similar legislation.

The Court rejected the argument that IRCA preempted the Arizona law.[3]

B. Finding the Workers

Now that the labor pool is limited to those authorized to work in the United States, an employer needs to advertise the job openings. Or does she? Sometimes employers hire through what is known as "word-of-mouth." This means the employer lets her employees know there are openings and the employees let their friends, acquaintances, and neighbors know. This is a very efficient and cheap way to advertise openings. However, if the workplace is already predominantly comprised of individuals of one gender, race, religion, age, or disability status, word-of-mouth hiring can result in a skewed workforce. As long as the employer isn't using word of mouth with the intent of discriminating, the method is not a violation of the anti-discrimination statutes.[4] Remember the ice cream store example at the beginning of the chapter? That would be considered word-of-mouth hiring.

Now, if an employer chooses to place ads for the jobs, another set of legal considerations arise. One new development in employment law involves salary transparency requirements. A number of states have enacted laws that require employers to include the salary range in job postings. The salary or hourly wage should be that which the employer reasonably expects to pay for the position advertised.

Where are the ads placed? How are they worded? Federal and state statutes prohibit discriminatory employment ads. A company cannot advertise for a "sales*man*" or a Christian accountant.[5] In

3 Chamber of Commerce v. Whiting, 563 U.S. 582 (2011).

4 For example, *see* EEOC v. Cons. Service Systems, 989 F.2d 233 (7th Cir. 1993).

5 There is a narrow exception known as the bona fide occupational qualification. This will be discussed in greater detail in Chapter 4.

today's world of internet algorithms and online job sites, employers may also run afoul of the law if job ads are posted in a way to limit the audience and screen out certain groups of people who are protected under the anti-discrimination in employment statutes (more about this in the next Chapter). For example, only showing Facebook ads to recent college graduates could be a violation of the Age Discrimination in Employment Act.

Additionally, as employers consider the labor pool, they cannot refuse to hire current, past, and potential future military service members due to their military service[6] or against job applicants who are currently unemployed.[7]

> ***Note on Nepotism***: Nepotism occurs when the employer chooses to hire friends or family. Generally, it is not unlawful, although many states prohibit it in public employment and businesses may prohibit it through an internal policy. Nepotism can potentially give rise to a claim under the anti-discrimination statutes if it leads to certain protected classes being disfavored in the workplace (but this would only occur if there were repeated instances of nepotism in hiring).

C. Applications

Employment applications typically ask for general information, education, and work history. The potential trouble areas occur when employers ask for demographic information and/or criminal background history. For demographic information, it is not unlawful for employers to request information such as race, religion, age, etc., on employment applications. However, having requested this

---

[6] Uniformed Services Employment and Reemployment Act, 38 U.S.C. § 4301 et seq. For example, an employer is prohibited from refusing to hire someone due to her possible future deployment.

[7] Several states prohibit discrimination against applicants who are unemployed.

information, employers may then face a claim when they choose not to hire someone. Although applicants must prove that the employer chose not to hire them due to their membership in the protected class, providing the information on the application sets the stage for a claim.

When it comes to criminal background information, states have a variety of laws that prohibit employers from requesting specific information. For example, California prohibits employers from requesting information concerning marijuana convictions more than two years old. Massachusetts prohibits most employers from asking about any criminal background during the application process. (More on this below). The chaos occurs when employers try to use one standard application across multiple states and then throw in some disclaimers to attempt to limit their liability. For example, on the first page of an application, a question asks, "have you ever been arrested?" Then, at the bottom of the third page, the application states "If you are a resident of Massachusetts, you do not need to answer the question about arrests." This example application is problematic because any use of disclaimers must be clearly understandable to the average reader, and the disclaimer must be near to the question itself (as opposed to being buried at the end of the application).

D. Interviews

Many people believe that federal law prevents employers from asking certain questions in interviews—such as demographic information or whether an applicant is pregnant or planning to become pregnant. However, under federal law, asking these questions is not unlawful per se. Similar to the job application, however, the employer has put itself in a vulnerable position if they ask these questions and then don't hire the applicant.

You know what's coming, right? Yup—under state law, some states prohibit asking questions concerning protected status (anyone covered by an anti-discrimination statute). And further, under some state common law, potential employees are protected from termination when they lie in response to an unlawful question. To illustrate this concept, suppose your partner is pregnant when you interview for a job. If you voluntarily offer false information, without being asked directly, you aren't protected from termination for lying ("I will never need paternity leave because I'm never having children!"). But if the employer asks you an unlawful question ("so, are you ever going to need paternity leave?") and you answer falsely ("No, nope, never"), then you are protected.

> ***Note on Accommodations***: Asking an applicant about their need for an accommodation due to a religious belief or disability is appropriate because the employer has an obligation to provide accommodations on these grounds.[8]

E. Pre-Employment Screenings and Background Checks

Often the last step before being hired is some type of screening. This can be a criminal background check, a drug test, or in some cases, a physical exam. Dealing with criminal background checks, many states and cities have "Ban the BOX" legislation which prohibits an employer from asking about criminal backgrounds (as discussed above) on applications but still allows employers to check an applicant's criminal history after an interview. You should check for your jurisdiction.

Despite state law playing a large role in governing the screening process, federal law is relevant in a few ways. First, when the federal government is acting as an employer, the Supreme Court

---

[8] See Chapter 4 for more information on accommodations.

held that reasonable, employment-related inquiries that further the government's interest in managing its internal operations do not violate any right to privacy.[9] Further, when asking a job-related question, the government doesn't have to prove that the questions are necessary, just that they are reasonable. For example, employees at NASA's jet propulsion lab challenged the federal government's request, as employer, for information about past drug use and participation in drug treatment programs. Employees argued that requesting this information was a violation of the right to informational privacy. The Court held that asking about drug use, for super fancy jet propulsion lab employees, is reasonable to make sure that employees are able to carry out their job duties.

Finally, the Americans with Disabilities Act ("ADA") explicitly discusses pre-employment medical inquiries or tests. Employers are allowed to condition offers of employment on the results of a medical exam but only if all applicants are required to take the exam and if the results are kept confidential. Further, the ADA explicitly removes drug screenings from this requirement.

F. References

There are a few different legal considerations with references. First, if the prior employer provides a false or incomplete reference and that causes injury to a third party, is the prior employer subject to liability? Second, if the prior employer provides a reference that contains false information to the detriment of the applicant, can the applicant bring an action against the prior employer?

Consider the following scenarios:

- Employer A, when asked for a reference for Joe by Employer B, failed to disclose that Joe fell asleep while driving and caused an accident. If Employer B

[9] NASA v. Nelson, 562 U.S. 134 (2011).

then hires Joe and Joe falls asleep and causes an accident, may Employer B recover against Employer A?

- Employer B never bothered to check references with Employer A and Joe fell asleep and injured someone—may the injured party bring an action against Employer B?
- Joe was in fact a model employee and never caused any problems, but Employer A gave Joe a bad reference which caused Employer B not to hire him. May Joe recover against Employer A?

Tort claims against the prior employer may include *negligent misrepresentation* or *intentional misrepresentation*. The contours of these claims will depend on state law, of course, and will also turn on whether the prior employer provided false or misleading answers. In some states, employers don't have an affirmative duty to disclose information in a reference check unless there is a fiduciary or confidential relationship.[10] In other words, if the previous employer responds to a request for information by merely confirming the dates of employment, this "silence" will not be unlawful unless the previous employer had a fiduciary duty to disclose other information.

Closely related to these claims of misrepresentation are claims for *negligent hiring*. Many of the leading cases which you may find in your casebook involve long-haul truckers. For example, the employer hires a long-haul trucker without checking his criminal background and provides a truck with a sleeping compartment. The trucker has past criminal convictions for sexually assaulting

[10] You have probably come across the term "fiduciary" in other classes. In this context, it simply means that the previous employer has an obligation to provide more information than most employers. More generally, it means a person who has an obligation to act in the best interest of someone else.

hitchhikers in his truck. When the trucker does so again, the survivor of the assault brings a claim for negligent hiring against the employer.[11] Liability for failing to perform a background check will be dependent on the type of job at issue. However, there are higher standards for jobs working with children or other vulnerable populations or with access to living areas (like apartments). Courts employ a reasonable person standard and ask if the employer knew or should have known the person hired was unfit for the job, meaning that a third party is put at risk. Many cases ultimately turn on the question of foreseeability: would an investigation into the employee's background have made it foreseeable that the employee would engage in the action that led to the third party's injury?

Finally, if a prior employer provides a reference that contains negative information that causes an applicant to lose a job opportunity, that applicant may wish to bring a defamation claim against the prior employer. The success of the claim is dependent on the truth of the information provided. Many states have laws which set forth the type of information an employer may provide[12] and protect employers from defamation claims based on references, as long as the information provided is "truthful" or "in good faith."

IN SUMMARY: From who may be hired to how they may be hired, at every step in the hiring process, employers must follow federal, state, and local laws when choosing their workers. These laws cover topics ranging from anti-discrimination to immigration to criminal background checks. In addition, employers have obligations to check the backgrounds of applicants to avoid harm to co-workers and customers.

---

[11] Malorney v. B & L Motor Freight, Inc., 496 N.E.2d 1086 (1986).

[12] Information may be limited to job performance, reasons for termination or separation, or in the most limited circumstances, simply the dates of employment.

CHAPTER 4

Discrimination

Employment Discrimination is often what many people think of when they think about Employment Law. The doctrine in this area is pretty complex—it could be its own book![1] This chapter will give you an overview of the federal statutes and frameworks in the area of Employment Discrimination. Types of claims covered in this chapter include racial discrimination, religious discrimination, sex discrimination, age discrimination, disability discrimination, retaliation, and harassment. This chapter is just an overview of employment discrimination, so please know that many nuances and details are not discussed in this chapter.

In most courses, you will focus on the "Big Three" anti-discrimination statutes: Title VII of the Civil Rights Act of 1964 ("Title VII"), the Age Discrimination in Employment Act of 1967 ("ADEA"), and the Americans with Disabilities Act of 1990 ("ADA"). Title VII prohibits employers from taking actions "because of" an employee's race, color, religion, national origin, and sex. The ADEA prohibits actions taken "because of" age against someone at least 40 years old. The ADA prohibits actions against "qualified

[1] It is. It is its own book. *See* ANN JULIANO, A SHORT & HAPPY GUIDE TO EMPLOYMENT DISCRIMINATION (2021).

individuals" with a disability. One additional important statute is 42 U.S.C. § 1981, which prohibits discrimination because of race in the creation and enforcement of contracts (including employment contracts). But remember, as with all other parts of Employment Law, states and cities also have anti-discrimination laws. These laws may have additional protected classes or different definitions for which businesses count as employers. As always, make sure to check the state and local laws!

A. The Basics

We have already covered some of the threshold questions: who counts as an *employee* and who counts as an *employer*.[2] Recall that a business must have 15 or more employees to fall within Title VII and the ADA and must have 20 or more employees to fall within the ADEA. (To answer your question, yes, Congress did do this just to make your life more difficult.) Chapter 2 sets forth the tests for which workers count as "employees." Another critical question for these statutes is whether the employment action falls within the statute. (Did someone get fired or were you denied your favorite type of pen?

Hiring, firing, refusing to hire, paying someone less—these actions are unquestionably covered. After all, the statutory language prohibits employers from "failing or refusing to hire or to fire any individual." The statutes also prohibit discrimination in compensation. So, paying an employee less because of a prohibited reason is covered. The statutes, however, go beyond hiring, firing, and compensation decisions to prohibit "discriminat[ion] with respect to . . . terms, conditions, or privileges of employment." Courts have interpreted this language to require the claimant to

---

[2] Labor organizations and employment agencies are also potential defendants under these statutes. Private membership clubs and Indian tribes are excluded as "employers." Certain religious organizations may discriminate on the basis of religion. (More on this below).

prove that an "adverse employment action" occurred and the action needs to be materially adverse. "Adverse" doesn't mean the employer is cackling and acting with evil intent. Losing a promotion, getting demoted, being transferred with a loss in pay—these are all adverse actions. So, in answer to the above question, you probably cannot sue if your employer doesn't give you your favorite type of pen. Further, there does not need to be an economic harm. Because the statutes use the language "terms, conditions, and privileges" of employment, employers are forbidden from making the workplace a nasty place to work because of the protected classes.[3] This is known as a "hostile work environment," discussed below.

There is a separate employment action known as a "failure to accommodate" claim. Employers must accommodate religious practices, known disabilities, and pregnant workers. Accommodations involve reasonable changes to job responsibilities or structures. This is also discussed below.

> **IN SUMMARY:** Once you have decided if the workplace counts as an EMPLOYER, the individual counts as an EMPLOYEE, and the action at issue counts as a COVERED ACTION (e.g., *Widgets, Inc., with 100 employees fires Sarah, a full-time employee*), then you have to decide if and how Sarah can prove that they were fired BECAUSE OF membership in a protected class.

B. The Frameworks

The biggest question for anti-discrimination statutes is **how to prove a violation of the statute**. This is the focus of most Employment Discrimination courses. There are well-established "frameworks" that govern in this area, with prima facie cases and defenses unique to each framework. A quick way to distinguish

[3] If the workplace is hostile for reasons unrelated to a protected class (i.e., the boss is a jerk to everyone), it isn't a violation of the anti-discrimination statutes.

between the frameworks is whether there is intentional discrimination or unintentional discrimination. If the employer intentionally discriminated, the relevant framework is known as "disparate treatment." This might be aimed at one employee ("I'm not hiring you because you are a male") or it might be aimed at an entire class of people ("I don't think women make good truck drivers, so I won't hire them"). A different framework covers unintentional discrimination, such as when the employer has a requirement that is keeping a protected class from the job ("you must be 6′ tall to be a firefighter" would tend to keep women from the job). This is known as disparate impact. Each of these frameworks has its own sets of requirements and relevant defenses. Sometimes, there are multiple sub-frameworks within a single framework! Aaaahhh! Read on.

1. Individual Disparate Treatment

The first, and most common, framework is the **Individual Disparate Treatment** framework. This is the appropriate framework when an employee believes he has been treated adversely because of his membership in a protected class. For any disparate treatment claim, the plaintiff must prove intent (intent to treat differently, not evil cackling intent). In other words, the employee must show that the employer didn't hire her because she's female or that she was fired because she's Black. Within the individual disparate treatment claim, there are two different frameworks: 1) single motive (also known as **pretext**); and, 2) mixed motive. The phrase "single motive" refers to a case in which the litigation comes down to a but-for situation: the plaintiff must prove that but-for the plaintiff's race, she would not have been fired.[4] The employer will, of course, offer a reason for the employment action (failure to

[4] The Court in Comcast Corp. v. National Association of African-Owned Media, 589 U.S. 327, 140 S. Ct. 1009 (2020), held that section 1981 claims require a showing of "but for" causation.

properly fill out paperwork). Mixed motive refers to a situation where there is evidence that the employer had multiple reasons for the adverse employment action, one of which is the plaintiff's membership in the protected class ("you were late to work and you're Catholic").

a. Individual Disparate Treatment—*Single Motive*

Let's begin with the single motive framework. The Supreme Court developed this framework in *McDonnell Douglas v. Green*[5] and it is commonly (and often) referred to as . . . the *McDonnell Douglas* burden-shifting framework. The burden is on the plaintiff to prove a prima facie case ("PFC"). Traditionally, the five elements of the PFC are:

1. **Membership in the protected class**[6]

   For this first element, a plaintiff would simply allege: male, female, religion, race[7], national origin; over 40;[8] qualified individual with a disability[9].

2. **Qualified for the position in question**

   At this stage, the plaintiff doesn't need to prove that he is the MOST qualified applicant for the job. He just needs to show that he meets the minimum qualifications—that is, whatever qualifications the employer announced. If the plaintiff has been fired,

---

[5] 411 U.S. 792 (1973).

[6] A plaintiff does not have to be a member of a historically disadvantaged group. In other words, a sex claim could be brought by a man or a race discrimination claim could be brought by a white employee.

[7] 42 U.S.C. § 1981 prohibits race discrimination in the making and enforcement of contracts.

[8] The plaintiff needs to be someone over the age of 40 who is discriminated against in favor of someone younger (General Dynamics v. Cline, 540 U.S. 581 (2004)).

[9] This is the overall definition of the protected class for the Americans with Disabilities Act.

then he simply states that he was performing his job at adequate levels.

3. **Applied for an open position**

   To prove a claim that someone refused to hire you because of your religion, you must prove that you actually applied. As long as the plaintiff makes some showing of interest in the job to the employer, this is usually enough to meet this element of the PFC. Further, you must apply for an <u>open</u> position. If the case is a termination case, then this element doesn't apply.

4. **Adverse employment action**

   Even though the statutes use the word "discrimination," courts have interpreted this language to require the plaintiff to have suffered an adverse employment action. "Ultimate employment actions" will certainly suffice—not being hired, getting fired, denied a promotion—but they are not the only way to satisfy this requirement. A transfer might be an adverse employment action, depending on the details (was there a loss of pay? benefits? opportunity for trainings?). For example, working longer hours for the same pay has been considered an adverse employment action.

5. **Circumstances giving rise to an inference of discrimination.**

   Originally, the Court phrased this element as "the job remained open." It then evolved to include "the position was filled with someone outside the protected class." But what if the employer eliminated the position? Due to the myriad of possibilities, some courts have phrased this element as "circumstances giving rise to an inference of discrimination."[10]

If the plaintiff proves the prima facie case, there is a presumption of discrimination. The burden now shifts to the employer to "articulate" a legitimate, non-discriminatory reason ("LNDR") for the employment action. There are two parts to consider: 1) what does articulate mean and 2) what counts as a legitimate, nondiscriminatory reason. According to the Court,[11] "articulate" means that the employer simply has a burden of production. In other words, the burden here is not as difficult to meet as a burden of proof. The employer needs to produce some admissible evidence regarding the reason for the adverse employment action (the Human Resources Director could make a statement). The idea here is to raise the issue that the plaintiff was not hired for some reason other than his membership in a protected class.

The reason articulated by the defendant doesn't have to be related to the job. The reasons could be subjective (employee's personality) or nonsensical (employee's zodiac sign). In fact, the reason could be unlawful (e.g., "you're too old" in a race discrimination claim), as long as it isn't a reason based on the protected class at issue.[12]

If the employer doesn't offer a reason, then the plaintiff wins. Guess how often this happens? Exactly—never! Once the employer meets this super difficult burden (a little sarcasm for you), the

---

[10] Because the elements vary so greatly with each factual scenario (hiring v. firing; the position is filled v. the position isn't filled), some courts have simplified these elements to three: 1) plaintiff is a member of a protected class under the statute; 2) there was an adverse employment action; 3) in circumstances giving rise to an inference of discrimination.

[11] Tex. Dep't of Cmty. Aff. v. Burdine, 450 U.S. 248 (1981).

[12] Although such a statement would indicate a violation of the ADEA, a plaintiff may not be able to recover due to the procedural requirements for claims.

presumption of discrimination is dropped from the case and the burden shifts back to the plaintiff to prove what is known as "pretext." This means proving that the reason offered by the employer is not the real reason for the decision.

It's important to know that the plaintiff doesn't win just because he proves the employer lied about the LNDR. The Court has held that proving the LNDR isn't the real reason is NOT the same as the employer never producing an LNDR.[13] Instead, the plaintiff must prove that the employer acted "because of" a prohibited reason. In other words, proof by the plaintiff that the LNDR isn't the real reason doesn't mean the plaintiff automatically wins.[14] However, the plaintiff isn't required to have additional evidence beyond the evidence used to prove the prima facie case.[15] This is because the jury could believe that the plaintiff's evidence for the prima facie case plus the evidence that the reason offered by the employer isn't then real reason for the employment decision is enough to believe there is discrimination. But the bottom line is that the plaintiff must meet the ultimate burden that his protected class is the determinative factor in the employment action.

To repeat: PFC evidence plus evidence that the LNDR is false MAY be sufficient to prove that the plaintiff's protected class is the determinative factor in the employment action. What remains true is that the plaintiff must show that the employer had the requisite intent to treat him differently (and adversely) because of his protected class.

That is the basic structure for a **single motive** case:

1. Plaintiff proves **PFC**
2. Defendant articulates **LNDR**

---

[13] St. Mary's Honor Center v. Hicks, 509 U.S. 502 (1993).

[14] *Id.*

[15] Reeves v. Sanderson Plumbing, 530 U.S. 133 (2000).

3. Plaintiff proves **<u>Pretext</u>**

    a. i.e., the LNDR is a lie and the real reason (the determinative factor) is his membership in a protected class

b. Individual Disparate Treatment—*Mixed Motive*

The second way to prove an individual disparate treatment case is through the "mixed motive" structure. This type of fact pattern applies when the employment action is taken for both legitimate <u>and</u> discriminatory reasons. For example, suppose the employer tells an applicant, "You have a bad personality; plus, you are Italian-American. So, you know, we aren't going to hire you." A bad personality is a non-discriminatory reason, but the decision is also based on national origin. This is known as a *mixed motive* case. Here, the plaintiff has a lower causation standard and only needs to prove that the discriminatory reason was a <u>motivating factor</u>, rather than the stronger determinative factor. In addition, there is a possibility of the employer proving that, even without the discriminatory reason, it would have taken the same adverse employment action. This is known as the "same decision defense." Due to a complicated history of case law and statutory amendments, as of this writing, each of the three main anti-discrimination statutes has its own mixed motive framework.

In 1991, Title VII was amended to include the § 703(m) instruction stating that it is a violation of Title VII if a plaintiff "demonstrates that race, color, religion, sex, or national origin was a motivating factor" for the employment action, even if other factors also motivated the action. If an employer proves that it would have made the same decision in the absence of the impermissible reason, then the available remedies are limited (but there is still liability).[16] This framework does not apply to retaliation claims (see below for discussion of retaliation claims).

What about discrimination based on age or disability? The Supreme Court in *Gross v. FBL Financial Services, Inc.*[17] held that the mixed motive framework isn't available under the Age Discrimination in Employment Act. Basically, the Court focused on the absence of motivating factor language in the statutory text of the ADEA.

The Americans with Disabilities Act is, frankly, a bit of a mess. The Supreme Court hasn't squarely decided the causation standards under the ADA and the lower courts are split. There are three possibilities. First, cases must meet the "but for" causation standard as set forth in *Gross*. The trend in the circuit courts is in this direction. The rest of the Circuits are split between applying the Title VII framework (liability established at the point where the plaintiff shows the protected class was a motivating factor) and applying another framework known as the *Price Waterhouse* framework (liability is avoided if the employer can prove it would have made the "same decision," regardless of plaintiff's protected class").

---

[16] If a defendant carries this burden, then the court may grant "declaratory relief, injunctive relief, attorney's fees and costs but shall not award damages, reinstatement, hiring or promotion." § 706(g).

[17] 557 U.S. 167 (2009).

To view it another way:

Breakdown of Individual Disparate Treatment Mixed Motive Claims				
	Title VII 703(a) claims	Retaliation claims	ADEA	ADA
703(m) framework	Available	Not available	Not available	Unclear
PriceWaterhouse framework	Not available	Not available	Not available	Unclear

WHEW. That was a lot of information for something that is supposed to be short! I promise that is the trickiest framework! On to the next one. . .

2. *Systemic Disparate Treatment*

The **Systemic Disparate Treatment** claim addresses an employer who discriminates on a class-wide basis. As a treatment claim, the plaintiffs must show intent on the part of the employer. There are two methods to prove this claim: 1) a facially discriminatory policy or 2) a pattern or practice of discrimination.

a. Plaintiff's Case

The plaintiff's burden on a <u>facially discriminatory policy</u> is straightforward: the employer has a policy that discriminates on its face. The only thing the plaintiff needs to prove is that the policy 1) mandates or allows 2) actions covered by the statute 3) on the basis of a protected class covered by the statute. That's it, that's the entire prima facie case. In other words, you **must** [mandated] be a **woman** [protected class under Title VII] **to be hired** as waitstaff [actions covered by the statute]. At this point, the employer avoids liability only with a statutory defense (discussed below).

The second method to prove systemic disparate treatment is a pattern or practice claim. When there isn't a facially discriminatory policy but few people in the protected class are hired (or promoted), there might be a pattern or practice claim.[18] As courts have explained, under this type of claim, a plaintiff shows it is the employer's standard operating procedure to discriminate against the protected class. In other words, the plaintiffs must prove that the employer has the intent to discriminate against the protected class. Let's consider Widgets, Inc. and Black employees. When there isn't a facial policy, how can plaintiffs prove the employer's intent against an entire class? Numbers. Lots and lots of numbers.

The basic idea behind the numbers is this: there is a significant disparity between who has the job at issue (the current employees) and who lives and works in the surrounding area (potential employees). The presumption is that an employer who is NOT discriminating will have a workforce that is more or less representative of the population in the surrounding community. When the disparity is significant enough, that may be enough to prove a prima facie case of intent to discriminate.[19] For instance, the Supreme Court held that when the disparity is large enough, the statistics alone may prove the prima facie case.[20] Further, even when the numbers aren't quite so stark,[21] a statistical analysis may still meet the burden. That's the prima face case for a pattern or practice claim:

- protected class under the statute
- adverse action

[18] These cases are primarily litigated as class actions or brought by the EEOC.

[19] Int'l Brotherhood of Teamsters v. U.S., 431 U.S. 324 (1977).

[20] Hazelwood Sch. Dist. v. U.S., 433 U.S. 299 (1977).

[21] Stark as in drastic, not as in Arya.

- employer's standard operating procedure is to discriminate

b. Defendant's Rebuttal

Although not technically a "defense" in the burden-shifting manner of a defense, an employer may challenge the basis of the plaintiff's case. For example, the employer could argue that the plaintiffs should have used the applicant pool as the comparison group rather than the general population or that the plaintiff didn't narrow the comparison group to the people possessing the required license. In addition, employers sometimes acknowledge the disparity but then provide some reason other than discrimination to explain it: "Yup, that is one big disparity right there. But we aren't discriminating against women. We have a veterans' hiring preference and more veterans are men." If you read *Personnel Administrator v. Feeney*, 442 U.S. 256 (1979), in Con Law, that should sound familiar to you.[22] Or, "no, no, it's not us, it's them! Sure, there's a huge disparity but it's because women don't want these jobs." This is known as the lack of interest defense. If the plaintiff can prove the prima facie case, most likely the employer is going to assert a statutory defense.

Finally, employers may rely on a statutory defense. Title VII and the ADEA[23] allow for an employer to facially discriminate in hiring (yes, I do mean flat-out discriminate). Specifically, an employer can discriminate in hiring if it can establish that age (ADEA, § 4(f)) or sex, religion, or national origin (Title VII, § 703(e)) is a "bona fide occupational qualification reasonably necessary to the normal operation of the particular business." Whew, that's a mouthful! That's probably why most people just call it a BFOQ.

---

22 FYI—Title VII exempts veterans' preference policies from the statute.

23 The ADEA doesn't have an explicit BFOQ defense, but it does allow other standards and qualifications.

Because a BFOQ allows the employer to discriminate, the defense is limited to situations where the job qualification relates to the essence or to the central mission of the employer's business. So, unlike the legitimate nondiscriminatory reason from the individual claim, this defense must be necessary to the business. For example, requiring an exotic dancer at a club with female exotic dancers to be female would go to the "central mission" of the employer's business.

c. Voluntary Affirmative Action

One last issue specific to disparate treatment claims is voluntary affirmative action plans.[24] Because affirmative action plans consider race or sex or national origin in employment decisions, they are subject to challenge under Title VII. Plus, if the employer is a public employer, there are possible claims under both Title VII and the Equal Protection Clause. As the Equal Protection doctrine currently stands, race-based classifications by a state actor are reviewed under the strict scrutiny standard.[25] The strict scrutiny standard requires the government to have a compelling state interest for the classification and to use the least restrictive means necessary to accomplish that interest. Sex-based classifications are reviewed under a heightened (or intermediate) scrutiny standard, requiring an important governmental interest that is carried out through means substantially related to that interest.[26] In applying the "compelling" or "important" governmental interest prong, the Court has found the need to remedy past segregation by that governmental actor as a compelling state interest.

Unless you have been living under a rock, you know that the Supreme Court decided a case involving affirmative action in

---

24 "Voluntary" means that the employer adopted the plan in the absence of a court order.

25 *See* Adarand Constructors, Inc. v. Peña, 515 U.S. 200 (1995).

26 *See* Craig v. Boren, 429 U.S. 190 (1976).

education.[27] In June 2023, the Court struck down race based affirmative action in college admissions (except at military colleges) as a violation of both the Equal Protection Clause and Title VI (a federal statute that prohibits discrimination because of race by entities receiving federal funds). Colleges may consider how an applicant's background has shaped their life experiences but may not explicitly considered race. It is important to note that this decision is in the context of education. The Court has not yet updated its decisions in the employment arena.

If the challenge to an affirmative action program is brought under Title VII, there is a different test. In *United Steelworkers of America v. Weber*, 443 U.S. 193 (1979), the Court held affirmative action plans meet the spirit and purpose of Title VII. The Court attempted to balance possible liability to Black plaintiffs who were underrepresented at the workplace with possible liability to white employees for "reverse discrimination." To find the balance, the Court created a three-part test (shocking—a three-part test!). First and foremost, there needs to be an actual plan (not some idea Wanda in HR mentioned casually over lunch). Then the plan:

- must aim to remedy a manifest imbalance,
- in traditionally segregated job categories, and
- cannot unduly trammel the rights of disfavored groups.

The counterintuitive part of affirmative action plans involves the litigation process. In a disparate treatment case, the plaintiff will show the elements for a prima facie case (for example, "very few people of my race have been hired in the last few years"). The employer will offer up the affirmative action plan as a legitimate non-discriminatory reason (which sort of doesn't make sense since

[27] Students for Fair Admission, Inc. v. President and Fellows of Harvard College, 600 U.S. 181 (2023).

it is considering race) or offer the affirmative action plan as an alternative to explain the disparity. Then the plaintiff has the burden of proving that the affirmative action plan is invalid by proving that it does not meet the *Weber* test. This may seem like the inverse of what you would expect, but it is what the courts require.

> **IN SUMMARY:** There are two methods to prove a systemic disparate treatment claim: 1) facially discriminatory policy or 2) a pattern or practice claim. The BFOQ is the primary statutory defense, but the employer may offer another explanation for a lack of employees in the protected class. Employers setting aside test results to avoid a discrimination claim falls within a systemic disparate treatment claim as do voluntary affirmative action plans. Of course, to assert these defenses, they must meet separate tests set forth by the Court.

3. *Disparate Impact*

What about when there isn't intent, but the employer has some policy or test that keeps out a large number of people in a protected class? The most straightforward example is height. If an employer has a requirement that all employees must be at least 5′10″, this would keep out more women than men. A challenge to this type of policy is a **Disparate Impact** claim. Basically, an employer's **facially neutral policy** affects one protected class more than others and cannot be adequately justified by means of proving the statutory defense (discussed below).

Just as with the *McDonnell Douglas* framework, the burden-shifting shifting scheme. It begins, as always, with the plaintiff proving the prima facie case. After proving her membership in a class protected under the statute, the plaintiff must then identify a "Particular Employment Practice." This is whatever facially neutral practice is causing the protected class to lose out. The practice could be a test (physical or written), a height or weight requirement, or even a decision by the employer to promote employees based on the subjective judgment of supervisors. Basically, the plaintiff must point to the specific requirement that is the barrier.[28]

Next, the plaintiff must prove causation—that the employer's practice is causing the impact on the protected class. Finally, the plaintiff must prove that there is a disproportionate impact. Of course, the statute doesn't define what counts as "disproportionate." But the EEOC has offered some guidance known as the 80% or 4/5 rule. If the protected group is passing at a rate that is less than 80% of the non-protected remainder's pass rate, it will be regarded as evidence of adverse impact.[29]

As always, the employer may challenge the facts underlying the prima facie case. However, the more common scenario is that the employer asserts a statutory defense. For Title VII, the main defense is known as <u>business necessity and job relatedness</u>. The employer has a burden of proof to show that the requirement is related to the job in question and is tied to measuring successful performance on the job. This is different from the legitimate nondiscriminatory reason in the individual disparate treatment framework because it must be <u>related to the job</u> and it must be shown by a burden of proof. In that way, it is similar to the BFOQ

---

[28] There is one exception, known as—are you ready—"multicomponent system incapable of separation for purposes of analysis." Whaaaa? This means if the employer uses many different tests and the plaintiff can't tell which test is causing the problem (usually because the employer doesn't keep records), then the plaintiff can point to the "bottom line" of which employees obtain the jobs.

[29] For example, men and women take a test. Of the men, 75% pass; of the women, 25% pass. You are comparing the pass rates. So, the protected class, women, pass at a rate of 33% of the men's pass rate. Under the EEOC's rule, this would be evidence of disparate impact.

from the systemic disparate treatment framework.[30] However, the business necessity defense differs from the BFOQ defense in that a BFOQ defense is a more difficult test to meet.

Instead, courts describe the business necessity defense as requiring the employment policy at issue to measure accurately successful performance on the job. But the requirement doesn't have to measure job success perfectly. So, if the employer has a requirement that employees must be 5′10″, then the employer must prove that being 5′10″ will, in the typical case, set the employee up to be successful on the job.

As with Title VII, under the ADA, the employer must show that qualifications that screen out individuals with disabilities are job related and a business necessity. Under the ADEA, however, the employer has a different defense. The Age Discrimination in Employment Act allows for the employer to act based on "reasonable factors other than age (RFOA)." This defense is easier to meet than the job related and business necessity defense because the employer merely needs a "reasonable" explanation for the employment requirement. For example, the employer might assert that it wanted to raise starting salaries in order to recruit better candidates.

Finally, if the employer meets it defense, the plaintiff has one last chance to show a violation. This is the "alternative employment practice" stage. Here, the plaintiff is trying to offer some other way to meet the employer's goals without having the disparate impact. In addition, the plaintiff must show that it is reasonable to expect the employer to use this "alternative device." This means that the plaintiff must show that the new practice won't be excessively costly to the employer.

---

[30] However, the business necessity defense is easier to show because it does not need to be essential to the business.

IN SUMMARY:

Plaintiff proves:

- Protected class
- Specific neutral practice
- Causes
- Disproportionate impact

Employer proves:

- Business necessity and job relatedness (Title VII and ADA claim); or
- Reasonable factor other than age (ADEA claim)

Plaintiff proves:

- Alternative employment practice

Putting them all together

Now you know all about the three main frameworks! Students usually find it helpful to compare them against each other. Great news! I did that for you.

Individual Disparate Treatment (single motive)	Individual Disparate Treatment (mixed motive)	Systemic Disparate Treatment	Disparate Impact
Plaintiff (*burden of persuasion*) **PFC:** • Protected class • Adverse Action • Qualified	**Plaintiff** (*burden of persuasion*) **PFC:** • Protected class • Adverse action	**Plaintiff** (*burden of persuasion*) **PFC:** • Facially discriminatory policy OR	**Plaintiff** (burden of persuasion) **PFC:** • Protected class • Specific employment

• Applied for an open position • Circumstances giving rise to an inference of discrimination	• Protected class is motivating factor in adverse action	• Standard operating procedure to discriminate against the class	(neutral) practice • Causes • Disproportionate Impact on protected class
Defendant *(burden of production)* **Defense:** • LNDR	**Defendant** *(burden of persuasion)* **Defense:** • Same decision defense	**Defendant** **Defense:** • BFOQ (burden of persuasion) • Alternative explanation • Affirmative action plan	**Defendant** *(burden of persuasion)* **Defense:** • Business necessity (for Title VII and ADA claims) • 703(h) defenses • Reasonable factors other than age (for an ADEA claim)
Plaintiff *(burden of persuasion)* • Pretext	Ø	**Plaintiff** *(burden of persuasion)* • No burden shift **unless affirmative action plan.** Then plaintiff must show plan does not meet the *Weber* test.	**Plaintiff** *(burden of persuasion)* • Alternative employment practice

Let's also consider the defenses side-by-side. In order of easiest for the defendant to meet to the most challenging:

- **Legitimate, nondiscriminatory reason** ("LNDR"): could be anything; burden of production.
- **Reasonable factor other than age** ("RFOA"): ADEA only; burden of proof; must be reasonable.
- **Business necessity and Job related**: burden of proof.
- **Bona Fide Occupational Qualification** ("BFOQ"): burden of proof; must go to the essence of the business.

C. Retaliation

Imagine you told your boss that Betty, a co-worker, is harassing you. Your boss responds, "What? I can't believe that you would accuse Betty of harassment! You're fired!" The next employee that Betty harasses would be much less likely to come forward and complain. To keep this from happening (ideally), the Big Three statutes all prohibit retaliation either with explicit language or through judicial interpretation.[31] This is a very straightforward claim—at least framework-wise. Good ol' *McDonnell Douglas*, single motive, burden shifting applies to a retaliation claim. It's the basic prima facie case, then a legitimate non-discriminatory reason produced by the defendant, and finishing up with a showing of pretext by the plaintiff. Of course, the elements of the prima face case are different!

There are three elements to the prima facie case: 1) the plaintiff engaged in protected conduct; 2) there is an adverse employment action; and 3) the protected conduct caused the adverse employment action. There are two types of protected conduct: **opposition** and **participation**. It is important to determine

[31] 42 U.S.C. § 2000e-3.

which type of conduct is at issue because they receive different levels of protection.

Opposition conduct involves actions NOT part of an official proceeding (in court or before an agency) where the employee is explicitly challenging, opposing, or questioning an employment practice by the employer. For example, internal complaints, union grievances, or media statements would be considered "opposition" conduct. The employee must be opposing something unlawful under the statute to bring an opposition claim under the statute. In other words, you don't have a retaliation claim under Title VII unless you were opposing something that is a violation of Title VII. However, the employer conduct you are opposing doesn't have to be ACTUALLY unlawful. You just need a reasonable belief that the action is unlawful.[32] Finally, the form the opposition conduct takes must be reasonable. You can't burn down the workplace to protest discriminatory hiring practices and expect to be protected.

Participation conduct is conduct by the employee within some kind of official action, either with an agency or a court. To be protected, the conduct doesn't have to be as formal as filing a lawsuit. For example, "participation" covers testimony at trial or in discovery. Gathering information for pending litigation will be considered participation (unless it's sneaky stuff like stealing confidential documents). Participation conduct gets almost absolute protection. I say "almost" because some courts have refused protection for conduct that is in bad faith or makes false claims or statements. Unlike opposition conduct, participation conduct doesn't require a reasonable belief that the employer's action is unlawful.

Adverse employment action. The Court set the standard for what counts as an adverse employment action in *Burlington*

---

[32] Clark Cnty. v. Breeden, 532 U.S. 268 (2001).

Northern & Santa Fe v. White, 548 U.S. 53 (2006). The retaliation itself—the adverse action—doesn't have to take place in the workplace. For example, the employer could threaten to have an employee's immigration status out under review. It must be some action by the employer that is materially adverse and would have dissuaded a reasonable worker from making or supporting a charge of discrimination. So, taking away the cookies in the break room won't count, but taking away the ability to take every other Friday off would count.

Causation. The employee must prove that the protected conduct caused the adverse action. Of course, that means the plaintiff will have to prove that the employer was aware of the protected conduct.[33] The causation must be but-for causation. No mixed motive retaliation claims![34]

The burden then shifts to the employer to produce an LNDR. Nothing tricky here! "Your transfer has nothing to do with that letter to the editor you sent about our hiring practices! We had already planned to transfer you." Remember that the burden on the employer isn't as strong as a burden of proof. The employer simply needs to have some evidence that it already planned the transfer prior to action by the employee.

The burden then shifts to the plaintiff to show that the defendant's LNDR was truly pretextual for the defendant's actual discriminatory motive. Just as with an individual disparate treatment claim, the plaintiff may prove pretext with direct evidence ("That's it! You complained about Betty—off to Siberia with you!") or circumstantial evidence. A common method for circumstantial evidence is what's referred to as "temporal proximity," which just means that the protected conduct and the

[33] Some courts list "employer knowledge" as a separate element of the prima facie case.

[34] Univ. of Tex. Southwestern Med. Ctr. v. Nassar, 570 U.S. 338 (2013).

adverse action happened close in time. In many retaliation cases, this is all the evidence available to the plaintiff to prove retaliatory intent. In shocking news to zero law students, the courts are split on how close in time the actions must be, but within a few months will generally suffice to establish the inference.

Otherwise, that's it for pretext. No mixed motive claims![35]

IN SUMMARY:

1. PFC
   a. Protected Conduct
   b. Opposition or Participation
   c. Adverse Employment Action
   d. Causation
2. LNDR
3. PRETEXT (no mixed motive)

D. Religious Discrimination Claims

Title VII has several sections dealing directly with religion. First, religious employers are exempt from the prohibition of discrimination on the basis of religion. Specifically, Title VII states:

> This title shall not apply to a religious corporation, association, educational institution, or society with respect to the employment of individuals of a particular religion to perform work connected with carrying on the activities of such an entity.[36]

---

[35] There is also no such thing as a disparate impact retaliation claim. You must prove the retaliatory intent.

[36] 42 U.S.C. § 2000e-1(a).

There is also an exemption for educational institutions employing people "of a particular religion."[37] Note that these exemptions allow religious employers to employ people of a particular religion. In other words, the exemption applies only to discrimination because of religion. The exemption does not allow a religious institution to discriminate because of race or sex. (See below for discussion of the ministerial exception).

Title VII places an affirmative obligation on employers to accommodate the religious practices and observances of its employees. The employer must do so unless the accommodation would create an undue hardship.[38]

Traditionally the framework for proving a failure to accommodate claim was as follows:

1. Plaintiff must prove:
   - he has a religious practice or belief,
   - that conflicts with an employment requirement,
   - the employee requested an accommodation, AND
   - the employer refused the accommodation.
2. Employer then proves either:
   - it made a reasonable accommodation, OR
   - it cannot provide a reasonable accommodation because of an undue hardship.

That said, in *EEOC v. Abercrombie,* the Court seemed to create one unified theory for religious discrimination.[39] Refusing an accommodation, in the Court's view, is simply a type of discrimination because of religion. The lower courts haven't

---

[37] 42 U.S.C. § 2000e-2(e).

[38] 42 U.S.C. § 2000e-1(j).

[39] EEOC v. Abercrombie & Fitch Stores, 575 U.S. 768 (2015)

completely abandoned the traditional framework and are still sorting this out.

Turning to the obligation to reasonably accommodate, the employer must provide some manner of change in the workplace to allow the employee to engage in his religious practice. To meet this obligation, an employer does not need to select the reasonable accommodation suggested by the employee. In addition, the employer doesn't need to prove that the accommodation suggested by the employee would create an undue hardship. As long as the accommodation offered allows the employee to engage in her observance or practice, then the employer has met its obligation.[40]

An employer needs to prove undue hardship only if it is going to argue that it can't provide any reasonable accommodation. There isn't a definition in the statute of "undue hardship" (see, I told you it would be a theme). The Court recently overruled an earlier case to define "undue hardship" as substantial increased costs to the employer.[41] The accommodation certainly cannot require the employer to violate federal law or a collective bargaining agreement. Courts had found an undue hardship when the accommodation would result in other employees working less desirable shifts (weekends or holidays) more often. However, the *Groff v. DeJoy* decision requires employers to look to additional options to accommodating an employee's religious practices than simply stating that requiring coworkers to work overtime is an undue hardship.

Ministerial Exception. Remember that the statutory exemption applies only to discrimination because of religion. Under the terms of the statute, an employee could sue a religious

---

[40] Ansonia Bd. of Educ. v. Philbrook, 479 U.S. 60 (1986).

[41] Groff v. DeJoy, 143 S. Ct. 2279, 600 U.S. 447 (2023).

organization for discrimination under any of the other protected classes of Title VII or under the ADEA or the ADA. Not so fast!

It is now well established that the courts may not hear any discrimination claims if the employee in question falls within the "ministerial exception." The Supreme Court first adopted this standard in 2012 in *Hosanna-Tabor Evangelical Lutheran Church v. EEOC*, 565 U.S. 171 (2012) and later refined it in *Our Lady of Guadalupe School v. Morrisey-Berru*, 591 U.S. 732 (2020). This doctrine holds that if an employee at a religious institution is deemed to be a "minister,"[42] the Court will not hear the claim and the employer can discriminate against the minister on ANY basis covered under Title VII. The Court expanded the ministerial exception because it does not want to interfere with the Free Exercise rights of the religious organization. In other words, who is the court to tell a church who should and shouldn't be a minister?

The Court held it is the actual duties of a job that determine whether an employee is within the exception. "What matters, at bottom, is what an employee does."[43] Because the teachers were involved in educating students in the Catholic faith and inculcating Catholic teachings, the teachers fell within the ministerial exception. Therefore, the courts could not hear the teachers' discrimination claims (such as race, sex, or disability).

IN SUMMARY: Consider the following framework for analyzing religious discrimination and exceptions.

1. Is the employer discriminating on the basis of religion?
2. If yes, is the employer exempt from the prohibition of religious discrimination?

---

[42] This is defined more broadly than Christian religions who use the term "minister."

[43] Our Lady of Guadalupe Sch. v. Morrissey-Berru, 591 U.S. 732, 753 (2020).

a. Religious organization

b. Religious curriculum

3. If no, is there a BFOQ?

4. If no, is there an undue burden?

5. Does the application of Title VII to the employer violate the Constitution?

   a. Because the employer is exempt; OR

   b. Because enforcing Title VII violates the Free Exercise rights of the employer.

E. Sex Discrimination Claims

1. Sexual Orientation and Gender Identity

In *Bostock v. Clayton County*, 590 U.S. 644 (2020), the Court held that the prohibition of discrimination because of sex covers discrimination because of sexual orientation or transgender status. The reasoning employed by the Court makes clear that <u>any</u> discrimination because of sexual orientation or transgender is prohibited by Title VII. In other words, the employee does not need to show any special fact patterns or stereotyping.

2. Dress Codes

Even though many dress codes or grooming standards have different standards for men and women (and yes, are very binary), such policies do not violate Title VII merely because of those differences. In other words, even though these standards have facial differences based on sex, the courts have consistently held that there is no violation of Title VII. However, gender-specific grooming or dress codes which impose an unequal burden of time or money on one sex are unlawful.[44] The plaintiff will need to have evidence of the cost or time needed to meet the standard.

3. Pregnancy

Congress enacted the Pregnancy Discrimination Act of 1978 ("PDA"). The PDA amended Title VII and added two clauses. The first clause really just expands the definition of "sex:"

> The terms 'because of sex' or 'on the basis of sex' include, but are not limited to, because of or on the basis of pregnancy, childbirth or related medical conditions;[45]

By adding pregnancy to the definition of sex, then any actions because of pregnancy are treated the same as employment actions taken because of sex. The second clause of the PDA created all the confusion:

> women affected by pregnancy, childbirth, or related medical conditions shall be treated the same for all employment-related purposes . . . as other persons not so affected but similar in their ability or inability to work.

Courts read this language to prevent employers from treating pregnancy and related conditions less favorably than other medical conditions. Prior to 2023, employers had no statutory obligation to provide accommodations to pregnant workers. So, if a pregnant worker needs a desk job because she shouldn't stand on her feet, the employer had no obligation to provide this accommodation. Some protection for accommodations were created when the Supreme Court decided *Young v. UPS*, 575 U.S. 206 (2015). Under that decision, if the employer offers accommodations to some employees but not to pregnant employees, then pregnant

---

[44] *See* Jespersen v. Harrah's Operating Co., 444 F.3d 1104 (9th Cir. 2006).

[45] "Related medical conditions" includes abortion, in vitro procedures, and most likely breast feeding (although not all courts have found breast feeding to be covered).

employees could challenge the failure to accommodate under a somewhat convoluted framework. Because the *Young* framework required pregnant employees to point to a comparator employee, it limited to the number of accommodations offered to pregnant employees.

To fix this gap, Congress enacted the Pregnant Workers Fairness Act.[46] The PWFA only applies to accommodations and does not replace laws that are more protective of pregnant workers. Covered employers are private and public sector employers with at least 15 employees, Congress, federal agencies, employment agencies, and labor organizations.

Under the PWFA, employers must provide reasonable accommodations to a pregnant employee or applicant for known limitations related to pregnancy, childbirth or related medical conditions unless doing would lead to an undue hardship for the employer. Undue hardship is defined as significant difficulty or expense.

What type of accommodations might an employer provide? Well imagine you are pregnant at work—what might you need to continue your employment? How about uniforms and safety apparel that fits, light duty assignments, additional break time to use the bathroom (trust me, this is key), the ability to sit while working, and perhaps closer parking.

In additional to requiring the provision of accommodations, covered employers are prohibited from requiring a covered employee to accept an accommodation other than any reasonable accommodation arrived at through the interactive process or to take leave, whether paid or unpaid, if another reasonable accommodation can be provided. Employers also may not deny employment opportunities to a qualified employee if such denial is

---

[46] 42 U.S.C. § 2000gg.

based on the need to make reasonable accommodations or take adverse action in terms, conditions, or privileges of employment against a qualified employee on account of the employee requesting or using a reasonable accommodation.

Finally, as with all anti-discrimination statutes, employers are prohibited from retaliating against an employee for exercising their rights under the statute.

> **TIP**: If an employee is not hired or fired simply because she is pregnant, that is a PDA issue. If the employee is denied a light duty assignment because she is pregnant and has been advised by a medical professional that she needs such an assignment, that is a PWFA issue.

F. Harassment

Each of the three main statutes prohibits discrimination in "terms, conditions or privileges of employment." Courts interpreted this language to prohibit conduct when it alters terms and conditions of employment because of the employee's sex, race, age, disability status, etc. Harassment claims fall into two categories: with a tangible employment action (known as "**quid pro quo**") and without a tangible employment action (known as a "**hostile environment claim**"). A hostile environment claim can be created because of any protected class. However, a quid pro quo claim can only be based on sex.

Whether a claim should be considered a hostile environment claim or a quid pro quo depends entirely on whether there is a tangible employment action at issue. The Court gave us a list of the types of employment decisions that count as tangible employment actions:

- hiring,
- firing,

- failing to promote,
- reassignment with significantly different responsibilities, or
- a decision causing a significant change in benefits.[47]

If one of the above actions is conditioned on sexual conduct, then the claim is a quid pro quo claim. If it isn't conditioned on sexual conduct, then it is a hostile environment claim.

1. Quid Pro Quo

In legalese, a quid pro quo claim exists when sexual conduct is a condition of tangible employment benefits, including salary, promotion, and continued employment. In everyday terms, there's a quid pro quo claim when a supervisor says, "have sex with me or I'll fire you." If the employee agrees to keep her job, or if she refuses and then is fired, there is an actionable quid pro quo claim. If the employee says, "get lost,"[48] and isn't fired, there is no actionable quid pro quo (although there might be a hostile environment claim).

This isn't a burden-shifting scheme. The plaintiff must prove: 1) a supervisor 2) conditioned a tangible employment action on 3) submission to sexual conduct. There's no burden shift or defenses. If the plaintiff proves the three elements, the employer is liable.

2. Hostile Work Environment

First recognized by the Supreme Court in *Meritor v. Vinson*, 477 U.S. 57 (1986), a hostile environment claim applies in situations where there hasn't been a tangible employment action but the

[47] Vance v. Ball State Univ., 570 U.S. 421 (2013).

[48] Feel free to use your imagination to fill in other statements.

workplace is abusive or hostile because of the plaintiff's membership in a protected class.

The plaintiff must prove:

1. The conduct was because of their protected class;[49]
2. The conduct was unwelcome*;

- *This applies ONLY in cases of hostile environment based on sex. "Unwelcome" does not mean the activity was under duress. Instead, it means uninvited.

3. The conduct was severe or pervasive;

- Because this element asks if the conduct is severe OR pervasive, there might be an actionable claim based on one incident if the incident is severe enough (for example, a physical assault). In *Harris v. Forklift Systems, Inc.*, 510 U.S. 17 (1993), the Court provided a few factors to help determine if the conduct is severe or pervasive.
    - Severity of the discriminatory conduct
    - Frequency of the discriminatory conduct
    - Whether the conduct is physically threatening/humiliating
    - Whether the conduct unreasonably interferes with your work performance.

4. The conduct altered the work environment both objectively and subjectively.

[49] A hostile environment claim may be present even if the harasser and the harassee are in the same protected class. For example, in Oncale v. Sundowner Offshore Servs., Inc., 523 U.S. 75 (1998), the Court held that same-sex harassment may be actionable as long as the other elements of the claim are met.

- This means that the plaintiff must find the conduct to be hostile (the subjective test) and a reasonable person must find the conduct to be hostile and hostile enough to change the work environment (the objective test).

5. Employer Liability

- Remember that the statutes place liability on the <u>employer</u>, not the harasser. Employer liability depends on the organizational status of the harasser(s). We can separate harassers into two broad categories: supervisors and co-workers (which may also include customers or clients).

What's needed here is a chart!

	Supervisor	**Co-Workers**
Tangible Employment Action ***(Quid Pro Quo)***	Liability (yup, that's it. If the employee proves the elements, there's liability.)	Doesn't exist. Co-workers cannot take tangible employment actions against co-workers.
No Tangible Employment Action ***(Hostile Work Environment)***	Vicarious liability with an affirmative defense: a) the employer used reasonable care to prevent and promptly correct harassment AND	Employer is liable under a negligence standard if the plaintiff can prove: a) the employer knew or should have known about the harassment AND

	b) the employee unreasonably failed to use reporting procedures created by the employer.	b) the employer failed to take prompt remedial action.

Because liability may turn on whether the alleged harasser is a supervisor, who counts as a supervisor? In *Vance v. Ball State University*, 570 U.S. 421 (2013), the Court defined "supervisor" as someone who is "empowered by the employer to take tangible employment actions against the victim." Remember tangible employment actions are "a significant change in employment status, such as hiring, firing, failing to promote, reassignment with significantly different responsibilities, or a decision causing a significant change in benefits."

IN SUMMARY: a hostile environment claim may exist for any protected class under the statutes. A quid pro quo claim is based on sex only, and it only arises if it involves a supervisor and a tangible employment action.

G. The Americans with Disabilities Act

Buckle up. The ADA prohibits discrimination against "a qualified individual with a disability" from discrimination on the basis of said disability. A "qualified individual" means an individual with a disability who can perform the "essential functions of the job with or without reasonable accommodation." Let's break this down into two parts: 1) individual with a disability and 2) qualified.

1. *Individual with a Disability*

There are three separate categories within "individual with a disability."[51] First, an individual may have an actual, present disability. Second, a plaintiff might also have a record of such an impairment. Third, a plaintiff may be regarded as having such an impairment.

a. Actual Present Disability

There are three separate requirements for this prong. The first is that there is a physical and mental impairment. Under the regulations adopted by the EEOC, a physical or mental impairment includes "any physiological disorder or condition, cosmetic disfigurement, or anatomical loss affecting one or more body systems" and "any mental or psychological disorder." There are many specific details concerning impairments that are beyond the scope of a short chapter in this book!

Once you have identified the physical or mental impairment, you need to consider whether the individual is substantially limited by the impairment. Currently, the test for "substantially limits" comes from the EEOC regulations (there's no definition in the ADA itself—shocking). Under the regulation, "substantially limited" is an individualized assessment of whether the impairment limits the ability of an individual to perform a major life activity as compared to most people in the general population. More specifically, the impairment does not need to prevent or severely restrict the major life activity at issue.[52] You should consider whether an individual

---

[51] The ADA excludes certain things from the definition of disability. The following are excluded from the definition of disability: "transvestism, transsexualism, pedophilia, exhibitionism, voyeurism, gender identity disorders not resulting from physical impairments, or other sexual behavior disorders; compulsive gambling, kleptomania, or pyromania; or psychoactive substance use disorders resulting from current illegal use of drugs." 42 U.S.C. § 12211(b).

[52] The EEOC regulations make clear that, for some impairments, it should be easily concluded that certain impairments will at minimum substantially limit major life activities. Two quick examples are Deafness will substantially limit the major life

has a substantially limiting impairment without regard to mitigating measures UNLESS the mitigating measures are glasses or contacts. For example, if the high individual has high blood pressure and is taking medication, what limitations would the individual face without their medication? In that case, Congress decreed, consider the glasses or contacts. (Look around at your classmates and you will understand why Congress made this exception). Finally, an impairment that is in remission (or episodic) will be considered a disability if it would substantially limit a major life activity when active.[53]

To be within the protected class, an individual only needs to be substantially limited in one major life activity. (She could, of course, be limited in more than one.) There is a list of activities in the ADA that meet the test:

> caring for oneself, performing manual tasks, seeing, hearing, eating, sleeping, walking, standing, lifting, bending, speaking, breathing, learning, reading, concentrating, thinking, communicating, and working.[54]

Further, the ADA now lists "major bodily functions" as a major life activity.[55] This means that impairments such as diabetes may substantially limit the major life activity of the functioning of the endocrine system and therefore may be considered a disability.

In the activity of performing manual tasks, the Court has held that the manual tasks must be "central to daily life," not simply specialized tasks for the job at issue. In other words, many smaller tasks cannot be aggregated together to equal a major life activity.

---

activity of hearing and Blindness will substantially limit the major life activity of seeing. 29 C.F.R. 1630.2(j)(3)(iii).

[53] 42 U.S.C. § 12102(4)(D).

[54] 42 U.S.C. § 12102(2)(A).

[55] 42 U.S.C. § 12102(2)(B). This includes "functions of the immune system, normal cell growth, digestive, bowel, bladder, neurological, brain, respiratory, circulatory, endocrine, and reproductive functions."

IN SUMMARY: To prove an ADA claim the plaintiff must have a. . .

1. Physical or mental impairment that,
2. Substantially limits,
3. One or more major life activities.

b. Record of Such Impairment

An individual might fall within the protected class because he has a record of "such an impairment," meaning, a physical or mental impairment that substantially limits a major life activity. So what kinds of records are we talking about? Think employment records, medical records, hospitalization stay, and education records.

c. Regarded as Having Such an Impairment

The third way into the protected class is to be "regarded as having an impairment." This category is the broadest coverage. If an individual does not need a reasonable accommodation, he should proceed under this category (because he doesn't have to prove the substantially limited element).

The ADA defines "regarded as" to include individuals who can establish that they have been subjected to an action prohibited under this chapter because of an actual or perceived physical or mental impairment, whether or not the impairment limits or is perceived to limit a major life activity.

Under this prong, you might have an actual impairment which doesn't substantially limit a major life activity and the employer is acting against you on the basis of your impairment. Or you might not be substantially limited but the employer thinks you are. Or you could have NO IMPAIRMENT, but the employer thinks you do and acts accordingly.

As you can surmise, the "regarded as" prong is very broad and is intended to protect people who lose job opportunities because of employers' beliefs in this area. There are two restrictions to keep in mind:

- If you fall into the protected class because you are "regarded as" having such an impairment, you are not entitled to reasonable accommodations.
- Under the "regarded as" prong, transitory and minor impairments lasting less than six months are not covered.

IN SUMMARY: The protected class includes three categories. The individual presently has a physical or mental impairment that substantially limits a major life activity, OR has a record of such an impairment, OR is regarded as having such an impairment.

2. Qualified Individual

All the above—that's the FIRST part of the definition of the protected class for the ADA. To fully fall within the protected class, an individual must also be qualified. The ADA defines "qualified" as "an individual who, with or without reasonable accommodations, can perform the essential functions" of the job. If a function is not "essential," and the individual cannot perform it, then he is still qualified. Only the essential functions must be met.

The ADA states the employer's judgment as to what functions are essential shall be given "consideration," and further, a written job description is considered evidence of the essential functions.[56] Additionally, an individual is qualified if he can satisfy the requisite

56 42 U.S.C. § 12111(8)

skill, experience, education, and other job-related requirements. To determine whether a function is essential, courts consider the actual functioning of the job: is the function actually something an employee must be able to perform? This does not mean that the function is performed on a daily basis.

Once the essential functions have been determined, the concept of reasonable accommodation comes into play.

3. Reasonable Accommodation

Reasonable accommodation is considered in a few different ways. First, to prove membership in the protected class, an individual will need to prove that she is qualified. She might be qualified only after the employer provides a reasonable accommodation. Second, a failure to provide a reasonable accommodation is a separate violation of the ADA. We'll discuss that claim below.

So, what counts as a "reasonable accommodation"? First, keep in mind that costs to the employer may be considered in deciding whether an accommodation is reasonable. Next, you could probably make a list and cover many of the accommodations considered reasonable. It certainly includes making the building accessible to individuals with disabilities by providing things like elevators, ramps, etc. Reasonable accommodations also include job restructuring, part-time or modified work schedules, and reassignment to a vacant position.[57] Further, the provision for aides, readers, and interpreters are also reasonable accommodations.

Although the ADA mentions reassignment as a reasonable accommodation, in some circumstances, reassignments might conflict with assignments made under a seniority system. The Court

---

[57] VACANT. A vacant position. An employer does not need to kick an employee out of a position to make room for an individual with a disability.

has held that an accommodation that requires a violation of a legitimate seniority system is not a reasonable accommodation.

4. *Claims*

All the claims discussed in the beginning of this chapter are available under the ADA. There are a few quirks to keep in mind. First, for a systemic claim (either treatment or impact), the ADA prohibits using standards or criteria that have the effect of discrimination on the basis of disability[58] and "using qualification standards, employment tests or other selection criteria that screen out or tend to screen out an individual with a disability."[59] Second, retaliation is prohibited under the ADA by the statutory language. The provision is a little different from Title VII and the ADEA because it also applies to coercing, intimidating, threatening, or interfering with the ADA on behalf of one individual or another.

There are two additional claims under the ADA. First, associational claims. ADA protects certain relationships, and these are known as associational discrimination claims. In fancy terms, an employer cannot discriminate against someone "because of the known disability of an individual with whom the qualified person has a relationship or association."[60] Let's say Jane is a qualified employee. Her son has a disability, and the employer is aware of this disability. If the employer fires Jane because he has concerns about her son's disability (maybe the employer doesn't want to pay for health care for the son or thinks Jane won't be devoted to her job), then Jane has a claim for associational discrimination. Reasonable accommodations are not available for this type of claim. The only possible defense is a direct threat (discussed below).

---

[58] 42 U.S.C. § 12112(b)(3)(A).

[59] 42 U.S.C. § 12112(b)(6).

[60] 42 U.S.C. § 12112(b)(4).

Second, failure to provide a reasonable accommodation is a separate claim under the ADA. The employer has an obligation to accommodate the known physical and mental limitations of a qualified employee unless there is an undue hardship. The employee must show that an accommodation is reasonable and then the employer has the burden to prove that the proposed accommodation creates an undue hardship (see below).[61] The ADA envisions an interactive process for reasonable accommodations that involves a discussion between an employer and employee. An employee should let the employer know of her limitations and request an accommodation. Absent a formal request, if the employer is aware of a need, it will need to provide a reasonable accommodation.

> **IN SUMMARY:** The ADA provides all of the main claims plus a claim for failure to provide a reasonable accommodation and a claim for associational discrimination.

5. *Defenses*

Some of the defenses available under the ADA are the same as with Title VII. Just as with Title VII, if the plaintiff alleges an individual disparate treatment claim, then the employer may produce a legitimate nondiscriminatory reason. However, unlike Title VII, the business necessity and job relatedness defense applies to all claims involving screening standards or criteria, whether those standards are facially neutral or facially discriminatory. Further, there are a few defenses unique to the ADA.

Undue Hardship. An employer is not obligated to provide a reasonable accommodation if it would amount to an undue hardship. The statutory definition of undue hardship is an accommodation requiring significant difficulty or expense. This is a

[61] *See* U.S. Airways, Inc. v. Barnett, 535 U.S. 391 (2002).

much more difficult standard to meet than undue hardship for religious accommodation. Although the employee may point to the cost of the accommodation, the ADA requires significant expense (rather than de minimis for a religious accommodation). The burden is on the employer to show that the proposed accommodation is an undue hardship. The ADA provides a number of factors to consider, chiefly among them the size and financial resources of the employer. This means the same accommodation might be an undue hardship for an employer with 17 employees, but not for a 500+ employee company.

Direct Threat. Another statutory defense is "direct threat." A direct threat can disqualify an individual from proving he is qualified. The ADA defines direct threat as a significant risk to the health and safety of other individuals in the workplace. The assessment must be made on the basis of objective medical judgment. The ADA provides factors to consider in deciding if an impairment is a direct threat:

- Duration of the Risk
- Nature and Potential Harm
- Likelihood of Potential Harm
- Imminence of the Potential Harm

Despite the wording of the defense—"direct threat to the health and safety of others"—the Court upheld an EEOC interpretation that expanded the defense to the health of the employee herself. *Chevron, U.S.A. Inc. v. Echazabal*, 536 U.S. 73 (2002). In other words, if the job at issue would pose a health risk to the employee because of her physical impairment, then the employer may consider the employee working at the job as a direct threat to herself.

IN SUMMARY: The defenses available under the ADA are LNDR, business necessity and job relatedness, undue hardship, and direct threat (to self or others in the workplace).

H. The Genetic Information Nondiscrimination Act

Employers are also prohibited from taking adverse actions against employees on the basis of genetic information. The Genetic Information Nondiscrimination Act ("GINA")[62] covers employers with 15 or more employees, unions, and certain training programs and protects employees and applicants for employment. GINA prohibits the use of genetic information in making employment decisions including prohibiting employers from requesting, requiring, or purchasing genetic information. There are strict rules covering the disclosure of genetic information.

"Genetic information" probably sounds very formal. And it can include scientific information such as employee's genetic tests and genetic tests of their family. However, the statute also covers family medical history. You know, those questions you are asked at the doctor's office—"has anyone in your family had a heart condition?"

That said, there are exceptions. An employer may obtain genetic information if it is obtained as part of health or genetic services offered by the employer on a voluntary basis (such as a wellness program). Further, if an employee is asking for FMLA leave, the employer may acquire information concerning the employee or family member's health condition.

I. Remedies

The big idea here is to make a successful plaintiff whole, to put him in the position he would have been in but for the

[62] 42 U.S.C. § 2000ff.

discrimination. This is sometimes called “make whole relief.” The remedies can be grouped into two broad categories: equitable relief and legal relief.

1. Equitable

The statutes all provide for various types of equitable relief, such as reinstatement, seniority, and hiring. When courts award this type of relief, they consider the current employees and try to avoid displacing or bumping current workers.

Backpay is the equitable remedy that really packs a punch. Because the Court considers this an equitable type of relief, the determination of back pay is decided by the Court and isn’t subject to the cap discussed below. It’s available under Title VII, ADA, FMLA, and the Equal Pay Act.

In *Albemarle Paper Co. v. Moody*, 422 U.S. 405 (1975), the Court held that although backpay is not mandatory or automatic, when considering the purposes of the Act, there is a presumption of back pay. Backpay doesn’t just mean wages. Backpay includes all the compensation a successful plaintiff would have received in the absence of discrimination (wages, raises, overtime, benefits, vacation pay, retirement benefits, etc. etc. etc.!). Plus, the backpay award comes with prejudgment interest from the date of the unlawful employment action. This can be a HUGE amount of money.

There are some limits on backpay. Backpay starts on the date the plaintiff first lost wages but can’t go back more than two years prior to the filing of a charge. The time period stops typically on the date of judgment but it might be stopped by other events.[63] Further,

[63] The backpay period can stop if the plaintiff resigns or turns down offer of reinstatement or dies or would have been laid off. It can also be cut off by something known as “after acquired evidence.” This means the employer fired the plaintiff because of his religion. Then, AFTER that decision, the employer finds evidence that the plaintiff was stealing from the employer. Because the employer didn’t know this

the backpay amount will be reduced by any wages that the plaintiff did earn and an amount that the plaintiff could have earned with "reasonable diligence." In other words, the plaintiff has to go get a job and try and make some money.

Front pay is another remedy available. It's a little wacky. Imagine that the court says you are entitled to reinstatement but there is no vacancy; front pay carries you over until you get the position. But if reinstatement is never possible (because the employer and the plaintiff hate each other), then front pay is damages in lieu of reinstatement. Because make whole relief is the guiding principle, the front pay calculation can be pretty complex. A front pay can include total future salary, pension benefits (etc. etc. etc.) from date of judgment until the probable loss of job or retirement! Just as with backpay, there is a duty to mitigate. A front pay award will be reduced by the amount the plaintiff will earn in whatever job she has secured.

2. *Legal Relief*

Compensatory and punitive damages are available under Title VII and ADA claims (but not the ADEA or the Equal Pay Act). These damages are available for intentional discrimination claims only (i.e. treatment claims and only as long as the employer hasn't proven the "same decision" defense) and Congress added a cap on damages based on the number of employees.[64]

$50,000 for employers with 15-100 employees

$100,000 for employers with 101-200 employees

---

at the time of the decision to fire the plaintiff, it is still liable but the remedies are limited.

[64] Because backpay and front pay aren't considered compensatory damages, these amounts don't fall under the cap.

$200,000 for employers with 201-500 employees

$300,000 for employers with 501 or more employees

What counts as compensatory damages? Many, many things: mental distress; lost earning capacity; inconvenience; medical expenses; the costs of looking for new employment, (etc. etc. etc.). Punitive damages are available when some agent of the employer acted with "malice or reckless indifference to the federally protected rights" of the plaintiff and the employer is liable for that person's actions. *Kolstad v. American Dental Association*, 527 U.S. 526 (1999). This means that there is a good faith defense is available to a punitive damages claim.

3. *Liquidated Damages*

Liquidated damages means the statute has set the amount. Liquidated damages are the amount of the unpaid (or lost) wages. A successful plaintiff gets double backpay. The Equal Pay Act and the FMLA automatically award liquidated damages and the ADEA allows an award if the violation of the statute was "willful." If a willful violation is proven, the liquidated damages MUST be awarded. A violation is willful if the employer knew or was reckless that its action violated the statute.

4. *Attorney's Fees*

Fees may be awarded to a "prevailing party." They are almost always awarded to a prevailing plaintiff.[65] This means the plaintiff won some judgment from the court (even if just nominal damages). A successful defendant might be awarded fees but it will need to show that the plaintiff's action was frivolous, unreasonable, or without foundation.

[65] In fact, the ADEA allows a fee award to plaintiffs only.

J. Quick Note on Procedures

Bringing one of these claims to court is a complicated process involving a state agency (most of the time), a federal agency, and finally, the court![66] To make matters more confusing, the time limits for filing are SHORT! Title VII is the standard (the ADA explicitly looks to Title VII for the procedures). The ADEA has some important differences[67] and federal employees have a different process. Although this may seem a bit mind-numbing, these administrative procedures have prevented more plaintiffs from suing on their claims than the substantive law. So, we better figure this out. Here are the basics steps:

1. File a charge with a state agency (if the state has one);
2. File charge with EEOC within the time period;
3. EEOC serves notice on the employer;
4. EEOC investigates and reaches a determination;
5. Charging party requests a Right to Sue letter (or waits for the EEOC to decide what to do);
6. File complaint in state or federal court.

I know this is quite a lot of information. Many, many nuances are not addressed here. If you are studying Employment Discrimination as its own subject, I encourage you to explore other sources for a fuller picture of these statutes and their frameworks.

---

[66] 42 U.S.C. § § 1981 and 1983 and the Equal Pay Act do not have these administrative requirements.

[67] The remedial provisions of the Fair Labor Standards Act apply to ADEA action.

CHAPTER 5

Wages & Hours

Think back to the first time you applied for a job. Surely some of your initial questions (at least to yourself) were "what am I getting paid?," "what are my hours?," and "do I get anything else?" In addition to your paycheck, you may receive benefits that are required by state or federal law—things like worker's compensation or unemployment benefits.[1] Employers also provide other benefits that aren't required by law, such as vacation time or tuition reimbursement. These additional benefits could be provided in an effort to keep a happy workforce, or due to contracts like collective bargaining agreements.

A. Fair Labor Standards Act

In 1938, Congress enacted the Fair Labor Standards Act ("FLSA") in an effort to provide minimum wages, to encourage employers to hire more workers by requiring overtime pay,[2] and to regulate child labor.[3] According to the Department of Labor, FLSA

[1] See Chapters 7 and 11.

[2] The idea here is that employers would spread the hours around more workers instead of paying overtime to a smaller number of workers.

[3] Employing minors is discussed in Chapter 2.

covers 143 million workers. Many of these workers will also be covered under state laws that regulate wages and hours because FLSA doesn't preempt state law.

As with so many of the employment law statutes, there are many, many specific questions and exceptions and nuances and . . . and . . . and. To impose some order in this area, consider approaching a FLSA question in the following steps:

1. Does this business fall within FLSA?
2. Do any employees fall under FLSA?
3. Are any of those employees exempt?
4. What must the non-exempt employees be paid?
5. How do I know which hours count as "hours worked"?
6. What about "Equal Pay"?

1. Does This Business Fall Within FLSA?

FLSA applies to private businesses with an annual revenue of not less than $500,000 which meet the definition of "an enterprise engaged in commerce or the production of goods for commerce."[4] Let's break that down.

Commerce: This commerce test applies to a business having workers engaged in interstate commerce, producing goods for interstate commerce, or handling, selling, or otherwise working on goods or materials that have been moved in or produced for such commerce by any person. This is a very broad test. My friends, this means if an employee is sorting supplies produced through interstate commerce, they are covered.

Enterprise: The term "enterprise" might conjure up an image of a vast operation. However, Congress was trying to reach the type

4 29 U.S.C. 203(r).

of business organization with multiple, smaller operations. Therefore, in order to meet this definition, the business must earn more than $500,000 or more in gross revenue and perform (1) related activities under (2) unified operations or common control for (3) common business purpose. For example, a company owns five hotels or a hotel with an adjoining restaurant. The five hotels would be considered an "enterprise" for FLSA purposes. There are two other categories of businesses which are included. First, public agencies are included. Second, certain industries are included, such as hospitals and schools.[5]

As you can see, the enterprise test is very broad and covers all employees who work for a business that falls within the enterprise definition. However, due to the annual gross profit requirement of $500,000, small businesses are exempt from the definition of enterprise.

FLSA also applies to Federal, state, and local governments.

2. *Do Any Employees Fall Under FLSA?*

To begin, FLSA covers "employees," defined as "any individual employed by the employer."[6] Yup, you read that correctly. Even if a business does not qualify as an enterprise, the individual workers at a business may fall within the protections of FLSA. Sometimes referred to as the "individual employee test," FLSA applies to an individual worker engaged in commerce or a worker who is engaged in the production of goods for interstate commerce. Remember, this test is very broad. However, a worker at a location where goods or

---

5 More specifically, businesses "engaged in the operation of a hospital, an institution primarily engaged in the care of the sick, the aged, or the mentally ill who reside on the premises; a school for mentally or physically disabled or gifted children; a preschool, an elementary or secondary school, or an institution of higher education (whether operated for profit or not for profit)." 29 U.S.C. § 203(r)(2)(a).

6 Recall from Chapter 2 that the Court adopted the "economic realities" test for the definition of employee.

services produced by the employer cross state lines even if that worker isn't involved in creating the goods will also be covered.

Keep in mind that although FLSA applies to employees of state and local governments, state workers cannot bring a claim under FLSA for money damages against a state unless the state has waived its sovereign immunity.[7] However, the Department of Labor retains the power to enforce FLSA against state governments.

3. *Are Any of These Employees Exempt?*

Then, you must consider whether the employee is exempt. There are a TON of exemptions in FLSA. Some are very specific (e.g., "professional crabbers") and some are more general categories that courts must then determine if a particular employee falls within the category (e.g., "computer industry employees"). Further, some of the exemptions exempt workers from the overtime provisions but not the minimum wage provisions[8] and some of the exemptions exempt workers from both overtime and minimum wage provisions.[9]

The largest exemption is FLSA Section 13(a)(1) which exempts "any employee employed in a bona fide executive, administrative, or professional capacity . . . or in the capacity of outside salesman" and certain computer industry employees. These exemptions are sometimes called the "white collar exemptions." For the first three categories, to be exempt the worker must (1) be paid on a salary basis (known as the "salary basis test")[10] (2) not earn less that a set amount, currently $844 per week as of July 1, 2024 and increasing to $1128 as of January 1, 2025 (known as the "salary limit test");

---

[7] *See* Alden v. Maine, 527 U.S. 706 (1999). This restriction does not apply to local governments.

[8] 29 U.S.C. § 213(b).

[9] 29 U.S.C. § 213(a).

[10] The salary basis test means that the employee must be paid on a salary basis—a set fixed amount regardless of performance or actual hours worked during the week.

and (3) the job must meet certain prescribed (known as the "job duties test").

In deciding if an employee fits within one of these exemptions, courts consider the employee's "primary job duties." Let's go straight to the source and see what the Department of Labor has to say about these exemptions:

> To fall within the Executive exemption:
>
> The employee's primary duty must be managing the enterprise, or managing a customarily recognized department or subdivision of the enterprise; the employee must customarily and regularly direct the work of at least two or more other full-time employees or their equivalent; and the employee must have the authority to hire or fire other employees, or the employee's suggestions and recommendations as to the hiring, firing, advancement, promotion or any other change of status of other employees must be given particular weight.[11]
>
> To fall within the Administrative exemption:
>
> The employee's primary duty must be the performance of office or non-manual work directly related to the management or general business operations of the employer or the employer's customers; and the employee's primary duty includes the exercise of discretion and independent judgment with respect to matters of significance.[12]

---

[11] U.S. Dept. of Labor, *Fact Sheet #17B: Exemption for Executive Employees Under the Fair Labor Standards Act (FLSA)* (rev. Sept. 2019), https://www.dol.gov/agencies/whd/fact-sheets/17b-overtime-executive.

[12] U.S. Dept. of Labor, *Fact Sheet #17C: Exemption for Administrative Employees Under the Fair Labor Standards Act (FLSA)* (rev. Sept. 2019), https://www.dol.gov/agencies/whd/fact-sheets/17c-overtime-administrative.

To fall within the Professional exemption:

> The employee's primary duty must be the performance of work requiring advanced knowledge, defined as work which is predominantly intellectual in character and which includes work requiring the consistent exercise of discretion and judgment; the advanced knowledge must be in a field of science or learning; and the advanced knowledge must be customarily acquired by a prolonged course of specialized intellectual instruction.[13]

This means attorneys fall within the exemption as long as the employee is working as an attorney.[14] Employees who work as a computer systems analyst, computer programmer, software engineer or other similarly skilled worker in the computer field are exempt if their primary duty meets a somewhat detailed test (so I stuck in a footnote).[15]

The final broad category of exempt employees is outside sales. Perhaps you worked in sales before law school, or you have friends who work in sales. These employees are often on the road, away from the main place of business. This is the concern behind the exemption. To meet the exemption, according to the Department of Labor, "[t]he employee's primary duty must be making sales (as

---

[13] U.S. DEPT. OF LABOR, *Fact Sheet #17D: Exemption for Professional Employees Under the Fair Labor Standards Act (FLSA)* (rev. Sept. 2019), https://www.dol.gov/agencies/whd/fact-sheets/17d-overtime-professional.

[14] There is a fun case discussing whether document review counts as exercising independent judgment and therefore, the practice of law. Have you done a document review?

[15] The employee's primary duty must consist of: the application of systems analysis techniques and procedures, including consulting with users, to determine hardware, software or system functional specifications; the design, development, documentation, analysis, creation, testing or modification of computer systems or programs, including prototypes, based on and related to user or system design specifications; the design, documentation, testing, creation or modification of computer programs related to machine operating systems; or a combination of the aforementioned duties, the performance of which requires the same level of skills. U.S. DEPT. OF LABOR, *Fact Sheet #17E:Exemption for Employees in Computer-Related Occupations Under the Fair Labor Standards Act (FLSA)* (rev. Sept. 2019), https://www.dol.gov/agencies/whd/fact-sheets/17e-overtime-computer.

defined in the FLSA), or obtaining orders or contracts for services or for the use of facilities for which a consideration will be paid by the client or customer; and [t]he employee must be customarily and regularly engaged away from the employer's place or places of business."[16] The Supreme Court held in *Christopher v. Smithkline Beacham*, 567 U.S. 142 (2012), that pharmaceutical sales reps fall within this exemption. It reached this conclusion using a "functional approach" to determine that the pharmaceutical sales reps have the indicia of salespeople even though they don't actually sell a product. Further, an exemption for these employees would meet the purpose of the exemption given that they earn high salaries and work irregular hours.

As mentioned above, there are a great deal of more specific exemptions: journalists on small newspapers; seasonal workers; "salesmen, partsmen, or mechanics primarily engaged in selling or servicing automobiles;" and highly compensated individuals,[17] for example. One area where there have been some changes is in the area of domestic service workers. Although some domestic service workers are covered by FLSA (the chauffeur who drove you to class today is covered), many workers are exempt. For example, causal babysitters[18] and companions to the elderly are exempt. The increasing rise of people who provide these services but are employed by third party agencies has created interpretation questions. The Supreme Court held that home care workers who are employed by agencies fit within the 13(a)(5) exemption.[19] The Department of Labor then revised its regulations to narrow the class

---

16 U.S. DEPT. OF LABOR, *Fact Sheet #17F: Exemption for Outside Sales Employees Under the Fair Labor Standards Act (FLSA)* (rev. Sept. 2019), https://www.dol.gov/agencies/whd/fact-sheets/17f-overtime-outside-sales.

17 To be considered a "highly compensated" employee, annual compensation must be over $107,432 (as of 2023) and the employee must regularly perform the job duties of an executive, administrative, or professional employee.

18 Some states or cities have enacted laws requiring certain minimum days of rest per week and paid days off per year for nannies.

19 Long Island Care at Home, Ltd. v. Coke, 551 U.S. 158 (2007).

of exempt workers in this situation to workers who are "elder sitting" instead of professional workers.

"Wait a minute? What about my unpaid externship????"

Many of you have undoubtedly worked as unpaid interns, perhaps for academic credit. Why don't these unpaid internships violate the FLSA? The short answer is that the Department of Labor and the courts look to the "economic reality" of the intern-employer relationship to determine which party is the "primary beneficiary" of the relationship.[20] Basically, the Department of Labor and the courts are weighing which party is benefitting the most from the experience—the employer or the intern. This is known—wait for it—as the Primary Benefits test. If the intern is determined to be an employee, then they must be paid in accordance with FLSA.[21]

---

[20] The oft-cited case as Glatt v. Fox Searchlight Pictures, 811 F.3d 528 (2d Cir. 2016) did just this.

[21] The Department of Labor cites to the following seven factors as relied upon by courts:

1. The extent to which the intern and the employer clearly understand that there is no expectation of compensation. Any promise of compensation, express or implied, suggests that the intern is an employee—and vice versa.
2. The extent to which the internship provides training that would be similar to that which would be given in an educational environment, including the clinical and other hands-on training provided by educational institutions.
3. The extent to which the internship is tied to the intern's formal education program by integrated coursework or the receipt of academic credit.
4. The extent to which the internship accommodates the intern's academic commitments by corresponding to the academic calendar.
5. The extent to which the internship's duration is limited to the period in which the internship provides the intern with beneficial learning.
6. The extent to which the intern's work complements, rather than displaces, the work of paid employees while providing significant educational benefits to the intern.
7. The extent to which the intern and the employer understand that the internship is conducted without entitlement to a paid job at the conclusion of the internship.

https://www.dol.gov/agencies/whd/fact-sheets/71-flsa-internships

B. Wages

The FLSA sets the federal minimum wage. Currently, that wage is $7.25/hour and $2.13/hour for tipped employees.[22] However, this is considered a floor. A state may set its state minimum wage at an amount greater than the federal minimum wage. As of this writing, 30 states have a minimum wage above the federal level, with Washington State as high as $16.28/hour. Interestingly, two states (Georgia and Wyoming) have a lower minimum wage of $5.25/hour for those employers and employees not covered by FLSA.

As for tipped workers, a worker who earns tips may be paid as low as $2.13/hour as long as that wage plus the tips would earn them the minimum wage. In businesses where employees pool their tips, the credit to the employer cannot exceed what the employee in question actually gets from the pool of tips.

One other category of workers may earn less than the set minimum wage—so called "youth workers." Employees younger than 20 years of age may be paid $4.25/hour for the first 90 calendar days of employment unless state law requires otherwise.

Contrary to popular belief, FLSA does not prohibit employees from working in excess of 40 hours per week. Nor does FLSA regulate a maximum number of hours worked in a day or days worked in a week.[23] Rather, it requires overtime pay for any hours worked in excess of 40 hours. The required rate is time and a half of the regular rate.[24] However, the compensation for overtime may come

---

22 29 U.S.C. § 201.

23 The FLSA also does not require many "fringe" benefits provided by employers—paid time off, sick leave, severance, extra pay for weekend, etc.

24 Determining the "regular rate" can be way more complicated than you might expect. In general, the total amount of wages divided by the hours worked provides the "regular rate." So, if a worker is paid an hourly wage, then the calculation for overtime pay is easy—it's 1.5 times the regular rate. Certain payments need to be excluded from a determination of the regular rate (such as bonuses or vacation pay). Next, certain "premium pay" amounts must be excluded (are employees paid more on Saturdays or holidays or are employees paid more after working 8 hours in a day). In

in a form other than pay. For example, a public sector employee may be compensated with time off.

One final issue in the area of wages involves credits for benefits provided by the employer. FLSA allows employers to credit towards benefits such as meals and lodging. However, these benefits must be of a kind typically provided by the employer, the employer must give notice of that the benefits will be credited toward wages, must be accepted voluntarily by the employee, and must be for the employee's benefit, not the employer. However, many states have laws that require workers to be paid in cash (which doesn't mean literally handing over dollars) so few very cases are litigated under this provision.

C. Hours

Now we know that employers must pay non-exempt workers overtime for any hours worked over 40 hours a week, we must ask the question, what counts as compensable hours worked? The number of hours worked by an employee is based on the specific workweek in question. Employers cannot average several weeks of work together to show that the employee has worked 40 hours a week.

In general, the hours that are considered "compensable" are those hours spent on "principal job activities" and incidental activities integral to the job. This, to no surprise, creates a whole host of issues.

Meals and snacks. What about your coffee break or having a snack? Or waiting for the staff meeting to start? This time is typically considered compensable, at least as long as the time spent on these activities is less than 20 minutes. Hmmm, you say, what about

---

certain workplaces, determining the regular rate of pay can be mind-boggling. All of the requirements and details are truly beyond a "short and happy" description.

lunch? That depends on a few factors like the time spent on lunch and whether you are stuck at your desk answering questions or able to leave for lunch. If your lunch break is over 30 minutes and you are able to leave the workplace, that time is not compensable. However, if you are working from your desk while you eat your yogurt, then that time is compensable.

On call. This area is even murkier than whether your coffee break is compensable. There are many different types of "on call." Is the employee at work and sleeping? Are they at home, answering phone calls? Courts look to the benefits and the burdens on the employer and the employee. For example, suppose the City of Brotherly Love was expecting a massive crowd due to a religious leader's visit, leading to concerns about the ensuing traffic problems. The City tells its firefighters that, during the visit, they are not allowed to leave the City after their shifts for fear they wouldn't be able to make their way back into the City. Are these "hours worked"? Because it is to the benefit of the City to have the firefighters close by, all the hours they are required to be in the City could be considered "hours worked." In general, courts look to see how the employee is able to use the on-call time. Do they need to stay at the place of employment? Are they able to sleep? Watch TV? Drink alcohol? Go to a movie? These factors and more can help determine whether time "on call" counts as compensable time.

Commuting. The time spent commuting to and from the workplace is not compensable as "preliminary" and "postliminary" activity. However, if the job requires travel during the workday, the travel does count as compensable time except for travel from home to the first location and travel from the last location to home.

Security screenings, temperature checks, and changing clothes. The COVID pandemic, as with everything in employment law, brought new scenarios to the question of compensable hours. In addition to new scenarios, such as temperature checks to start the day, other activities raise questions. If an employee has to change clothes to carry out their job duties (i.e., "donning and doffing" protective gear), should the time spent changing clothes count?

The Portal-to-Portal Act, 29 U.S.C. §§ 251–262 tried to clarify that "preliminary and postliminary" activities do not count as hours worked. In considering the question of whether time spent waiting to undergo screenings count as "hours worked," the Supreme Court held that only those activities which are preliminary and postliminary to "principal activities" of the worker are compensable.[25] Further, all integral and indispensable parts of the principal activities will be compensable activities. The activities must be one that the worker could not dispense with in order to perform the activities. The Court then determined that the post-work screenings were not part of the workers' principal activities and not compensable. However, when a worker is working with toxic chemicals, the "donning and doffing" of protective gear is an integral part of the job and therefore the time spent to don and doff is compensable.[26] So changing into a uniform when you arrive at work will not be considered compensable

Remember that FLSA does not preempt state laws in this area. States continue to also regulate in this area. Because there is often separate state law that employers must meet, hours that are not compensable under FLSA may be compensable under the state law. For example, in 2021, the Pennsylvania Supreme Court held that state law defined "hours worked" as "time during which an employee is required to remain on its premises."[27] Under this broader language, the Pennsylvania Court held that time waiting for bags to be searched at an Amazon facility may count as hours

---

[25] Integrity Staffing Sols., Inc. v. Busk, 574 U.S. 27 (2014).

[26] Steiner v. Mitchell, 350 U.S. 247 (1956).

[27] In re Amazon.com Inc., 255 A.3d 191, 203 (Pa. 2021).

worked and therefore be compensable under the Pennsylvania wage and hour law. The California Supreme Court reached a similar result in *Frlekin v. Apple, Inc.*, 457 P.3d 526, 529 (Cal. 2020), holding that security screenings, such as bag checks, are compensable time and the employer must pay the employees for that time. So the interpretation of the state law is completely the opposite of the interpretation of the federal law! Moral of the story—ALWAYS CHECK THE STATE LAW!

D. Remedies

FLSA allows employees who have been underpaid to bring suit to reclaim the unpaid wages. In addition, the statute provides for liquidated damages in the amount of the unpaid wages. The Secretary of Labor may also bring suit to collect the wrongfully withheld wages and may also seek an injunction against further wrongdoing. FLSA does provided that willful violations may led to fines and possible criminal prosecution.

E. Pay Equity

You may be wondering why the topic of pay equity was not discussed in Chapter 4 with the topic of discrimination. Well, the Equal Pay Act ("EPA") of 1963[28] is part of FLSA and was enacted prior to the enactment of Title VII. Interesting, right? It covers only wages and only prohibits discrimination on the basis of sex.[29] As part of FLSA, EPA does not define the covered employer by a minimum number of employees. Instead, it applies to those workers who are considered employees under the definitions discussed at the beginning of the chapter.

---

[28] 26 U.S.C. § 206(d).

[29] Technically it covers the "rate" of pay which means the statute covers wages but also bonuses, vacation pay, etc.

What does the EPA prohibit? It prohibits the employer from paying wages to employees at a rate less than the rate paid to employees "of the opposite sex"[30] for "equal work." What counts as "equal work?" Excellent question! The statute goes on to define "equal work" as "the performance of which requires equal skill, effort, and responsibility, and which are performed under similar working conditions."

1. *The Prima Facie Case*

The prima facie case is straight forward. The employee plaintiff must prove that:

1. Unequal wages paid;
2. Equal work performed; and
3. It is on the basis of sex

A plaintiff isn't required to prove intent. But a plaintiff does have to prove she[31] is performing equal work to the employee of the opposite sex (this person is known as the "comparator.") Again, equal work means the jobs require equal skill, effort, and responsibility. In *Corning Glass Works v. Brennan*, 417 U.S. 188 (1974), the Court held that the jobs don't have to be identical. Instead, the jobs should be "substantially equal." As for the requirement that the jobs are performed under "similar working conditions," the Court interpreted that language to mean "substantially similar."

When comparing the jobs at issue, the focus is on the actual job requirements. Attempted shenanigans like a different job title or job description won't protect an employer if the job is indeed the same. As mentioned above, a plaintiff needs to pick out a "comparator"—an employee of the opposite sex performing "equal

---

[30] Very binary, right?

[31] The EPA covers male employees paid less than female employees as well.

work" who is being paid more. This could be tricky in a sex-segregated workplace.[32] But the comparator employee could be a former employee (or even a subsequent employee in the same job).

2. *Defenses*

Once the plaintiff proves a prima facie case, the burden shifts to the employer to prove one of the four statutory defenses listed below. Whichever reason the employer uses as a defense, it must, actually, explain the disparity in wages.

- Seniority system: this defense is met as long as the system meets the requirements under Title VII.
- Merit system: this defense applies to objective measurements of job performance.
- Incentive system: this defense applies to a measured output system by quality or quantity.
- Other factor other than sex: this is the main defense![33]

As you can imagine, most of the litigation involving employer defenses focuses on what counts as a factor other than sex. Courts have rejected a few arguments. First, if an employer had previously set salaries based on sex and NOW sets salaries based on its past salaries, then past pay doesn't amount to a factor other than sex. Second, if an employer is paying women less than men simply because women are willing to work for less than men (i.e., a market forces argument), courts have rejected that argument. But economic profitability has been accepted. In other words, if one

[32] The EPA applies to employees working in the same "establishment" which leads to questions about how to define "establishment." For example, in a chain restaurant, each restaurant would be considered a different establishment.

[33] An argument can be made that showing that a factor other than sex is the reason for the pay disparity means that the plaintiff can't prove the prima facie case. However, the statute treats this as an affirmative defense and therefore places the burden of proof on the employer.

section of the workplace earns more revenue, then paying employees in that section a higher wage is a "factor other than sex."

If an employer pays a woman less than a man working in the same job because his prior salary was higher, is this a factor other sex? Courts had (HAD, I said) been unified in allowing prior salary to qualify as a factor other than sex. But recently, at least one Circuit court has rejected prior salary as a factor other than sex in all fact situations.[34] Rather, the employer must show that prior salary is somehow job-related. Stay tuned for how this develops!

If an employer cannot prove one of the affirmative defenses, then the employer must raise the wage of the underpaid employee (as opposed to dropping the wage of the higher paid employee). In addition, the employee is entitled to back pay and liquidated damages.

3. *Interaction with Title VII*

Because Title VII does cover terms and conditions of employment, compensation claims may be brought under Title VII. However, because Title VII doesn't have an "equal work" requirement and doesn't have the "same establishment" requirement, the Court held in *County of Washington v. Gunther*, 452 U.S. 161 (1981), that the proof requirements of EPA actions do NOT apply to sex-based wage claims. In other words, a plaintiff bringing a sex-based wage claims doesn't have to meet the "equal work" standards. Even if the jobs are not equal, if the plaintiff is able to prove an intent to pay her less because of her sex, then there is a Title VII violation. Courts are split as to whether a challenge requires a facially discriminatory system or whether a

---

[34] *See* Rizo v. Yavino, 950 F.3d 1217 (9th Cir. 2020).

plaintiff can prove a violation through the *McDonnell Douglas* burden-shifting framework.[35]

But (there's always a "but"), in a piece of legislation known as the Bennett Amendment, Congress incorporated the EPA defenses into Title VII. In other words, if the wages paid wouldn't violate the EPA, then the wages don't violate Title VII. The Court held that all four defenses from EPA are incorporated into Title VII. Keep in mind that "factor other than sex" is an easier defense to prove than "job relatedness" and "business necessity."

4. Comparable Worth

One last note. Comparable worth is the theory that jobs that are of the same value to the employer should be paid the same, even if it isn't the same job or an "equal job." An often-used example is comparing administrative assistants to custodians. One could argue that these jobs are of comparable worth to the employer and should be paid the same. Still, however compelling you may or may not find this theory to be, courts have rejected it under both Title VII and the EPA.

5. Remedies

Recall that the EPA is part of FLSA. Therefore the same enforcement provisions apply. If an employer is in violation, that employer may come into compliance by raising the wages of the underpaid employee. The EPA explicitly does not allow an employer to lower wages in order to meet the statute. So, as with minimum wage or overtime violations, an employee may bring a suit to recover back pay and liquidated damages in the amount of the lost backpay. The EEOC may also bring a suit on employees' behalf.

---

[35] For a full discussion of this framework, see Chapter 4.

IN SUMMARY: The Fair Labor Standards Act is a federal statute of broad reach that requires covered employees (only employees) to be paid minimum wage and overtime for any hours over 40 hours per week. FLSA provides a number of exemptions from its provisions. To be exempt, an employee must be paid on salaried basis, at a certain level, and must perform qualifying job duties. There are also specialized exemptions for particular industries. The Equal Pay Act is a part of FLSA that prohibits employers from paying workers performing the same job different amounts because of their sex. Employers have four defenses to Equal Pay Act claims, including one very broad defense for "any other factor other than sex."

CHAPTER 6

Healthcare

As with so many topics in Employment Law, the area of healthcare is a mishmash of multiple overlapping federal statutes, state laws, and private employer benefits. Let's address each federal statute on its own.

A. ERISA

First up is the Employee Retirement Income and Security Act of 1974 ("ERISA"). You may have heard of ERISA in relation to pension plans and retirement benefits. However, ERISA also covers private "employee welfare benefit plans."[1] These welfare benefit plans include such things as health coverage, accident coverage, disability insurance, unemployment insurance and other benefits such as tuition or childcare. ERISA preempts any and all state laws related to employee benefit plans except for insurance.[2]

---

1 Plans of a certain size are covered by the Department of Labor regulations and not state laws regulating health insurance.

2 Under the McCarren-Ferguson Act, ERISA does not preempt state laws relating to banking, securities, domestic relations orders, and generally applicable criminal laws.

The very first thing to keep in mind is that ERISA does not require employers to provide any benefits. However, once an employer chooses to provide a benefit, they must meet certain requirements. Sometimes, courts have to determine whether there is, in fact, a "plan." Of the many factors considered, courts look to see if there is some type of administrative scheme to run the plan. If there is a benefit "plan," employers must meet reporting and disclosure requirements, including the requirement that they disclose a summary of the plan description. Further, employers cannot discriminate against someone for the purpose of interfering with their benefits (i.e., firing someone because you don't want their pension to vest or because their benefits will have a high cost is a violation of ERISA).

Employees who are denied health benefits may sue for a violation of ERISA. Yes, this actually means that if your healthcare company denies a benefit, it is possible to sue the plan under ERISA. However, in determining whether ERISA has been violated, the standard of review at issue will turn on the amount of discretion the plan places with the plan administrator. The decision is reviewed under a *de novo* standard unless the plan gives the administrator or fiduciary discretion to determine eligibility for benefits or to construe the terms of the plan.[3] If there is discretion, then courts review under the "abuse of discretion" standard. The abuse of discretion standard is a much more lenient standard for the plan and therefore, a more difficult standard for the beneficiary to prove a violation. As you can imagine, there is A LOT of caselaw concerning whether the administrator has discretion. In the end, most plans include "magic words" providing the administrator with final decision-making in denial or approval of benefits.

---

[3] *See* Salley v. E.I. DuPont de Nemours & Co., 966 F.2d 1011 (5th Cir. 1992).

Hoping for more discussion about ERISA? Tune in to Chapter 11 for a discussion of retirement benefits.

B. COBRA

The next relevant statute is the Consolidated Omnibus Budget Reconciliation Act, also known as COBRA. You may know that COBRA allows individuals to temporarily keep the insurance provided by the employer after they have lost employment. In fact, COBRA applies to even more situations.

First, COBRA applies to employers with 20 or more employees who provide group health care benefits. Second, COBRA kicks in when there is a "qualifying event." Termination of employment for any reason other than gross misconduct counts as a qualifying event. So does divorce or separation. In other words, if your health care coverage comes from your spouse's employment and you get divorced, you are eligible for COBRA coverage. The same holds true if the employee holding the coverage dies. Dependent children are also eligible to keep their coverage even if the parent doesn't enroll in COBRA. And finally, you have 60 days from the qualifying event to elect to receive COBRA coverage.

However, there are two big "but. . . ." exceptions. First, COBRA coverage doesn't last forever. It ends when you enroll in another health care plan OR ends after 18 months[4] or 36 months[5] of coverage. Second, the employer providing the coverage is allowed to require the individual receiving the extended coverage to pay the premium for the coverage, up to 102% of the cost (that extra 2% is an "administrative fee").

---

4 For termination or reduction in hours.

5 For other qualifying events (e.g., death of employee, divorce, etc.).

C. HIPAA

Everyone has heard of HIPPA (the Health Insurance Portability and Accountability Act). HIPAA is the reason you have to sign all those papers when you have a doctor's visit. To focus on the Employment Law aspects, HIPAA regulates how a covered health plan shares information with your employer or with others (which they cannot do unless you agree), as well as prevents exclusions for pre-existing conditions. So employer benefit plans are covered because they are a health-based plan but the employer himself/herself is NOT covered. Which means, contrary to many people on social media, an employer asking an employee about their vaccination status or for proof of vaccination is NOT covered by HIPAA.[6]

D. Affordable Care Act

The Affordable Care Act ("ACA") (technically the Patient Protection and Affordable Care Act of 2010), also known as Obama Care, has many, many, MANY provisions. However, much of these do not relate to Employment Law so we are going to set those aside in the interest of staying Short and Happy.

Turning to the first issue—as always, which employers are covered by the ACA? The ACA differs in its requirements based on the size of the employer. Let's begin with employers with more than 50 employees. These large employers have an obligation to provide "minimum essential coverage"[7] that is "affordable."[8] In the alternative, the employer may be required to make a payment to the federal government for each of its fulltime workers. Further,

---

[6] HIPAA also does not apply to the grocery store telling someone to wear a mask.

[7] "Minimum essential coverage" means providing 60% of the cost of medical care and free preventive care.

[8] "Affordable" means 95% of workforce is able to afford it which, in turn, means the cost is not more than 9.5% of household income.

employers of this size have reporting responsibilities, including sending reports to employees and the IRS concerning the coverage provided.

Smaller employers (with fewer than 50 employees) have the option to use the small business marketplace to offer benefits to employees. The small employers must withhold an additional .09% of wages and compensation over $200,000. Further, if the employer has fewer than 25 workers, the employer may receive tax credits for offering health benefits.

As for the responsibilities of individual employees, the original ACA included what was known as the "individual mandate." Non-exempt individuals were required to obtain health insurance by certain date or be subject to a tax. The Supreme Court upheld the individual mandate as against a constitutional challenge[9] but Congress repealed the tax portion in 2017.

The original ACA included a requirement for contraceptives to be covered but included an exemption for religious employers. In *Burwell v. Hobby Lobby*, 573 U.S. 682 (2014), the Supreme Court held that this exemption applies to a closely held corporation if the regulation impinges on the sincerely held religious beliefs of the corporation's owners. Further, in 2017, the Administration issued new regulations that expanded the exemption to cover private employers with religious or moral objections to opt out of providing coverage and to do so without providing any notice. The Court upheld these regulations in *Little Sisters of the Poor Saints Peter and Paul Home v. Pennsylvania*, 591 U.S. 657 (2020). The Biden Administration has proposed new rules to remove the moral exemption but leave in place the religious exemption.

Objections based on religious beliefs have also been made against other provisions of the ACA. The ACA requires that most

---

[9] Nat'l Fed'n of Indep. Bus. v. Sebelius, 567 U.S. 519 (2012).

private insurance plans provide no cost coverage for a list of recommended preventive care services. In a case brought in the Northern District of Texas, several employers challenged this requirement on two grounds.[10] First, they argued that the government Task Force that creates the recommended services was created in an unconstitutional manner. Second, they argued that the requirement that health plans provide medication for the prevention of H.I.V. violated their religious beliefs and therefore violated the Religious Freedom Restoration Act.[11] The district court upheld the religious claims of the plaintiffs. As of this writing, the Fifth Circuit issued a stay on the district court's opinion.[12]

E. Family and Medical Leave Act

You are probably already aware that federal law (and some state laws) requires that employers provide leave to employees for certain health conditions or birth or adoption of children. But you may not be aware of the details. The federal Family and Medical Leave Act of 1993[13] ("FMLA") applies to employers with 50 or more employees and to public agencies and schools. Further, it covers employees who worked for employer for 12 months and at least 1,250 hours in that time. FMLA provides up to 12 weeks of unpaid leave for the birth or adoption of a child, to care for a child, spouse, parent with a serious medical condition or employee's own serious medical condition. A "serious medical condition" may be considered an illness, injury, impairment, or physical/mental condition

---

[10] Braidwood Mgmt., Inc. v. Becerra, 666 F.Supp.3d 613 (N.D. Tex. March 30, 2023).

[11] In order to prove a violation of RFRA, a plaintiff must show that (1) the relevant religious exercise is grounded in a sincerely held religious belief and (2) the government's action or policy substantially burdens that exercise. If the plaintiff meets this burden, the government "may substantially burden a person's exercise of religion only if demonstrates that application of the burden to the person (1) is in furtherance of a compelling governmental interest; and (2) is the least restrictive means of furthering that compelling governmental interest." 42 U.S.C. § 2000bb-1(b).

[12] Oral argument was held in March 2024.

[13] 29 U.S.C. § 2601 et seq.

involving inpatient care or continuing treatment by a healthcare provider. FMLA also requires employers to provide unpaid leave for family members of military service members—leave for certain reasons related to a family member's foreign deployment and leave when a family member is a current servicemember or recent veteran with a serious injury or illness.

What you may not realize is that FMLA does not require the leave to be paid. Further, your employer may require the use of your accrued leave that you have saved up. In other words, if you have saved three weeks of vacation time and one week of sick time, your employer may require you to use those four weeks as part of your FMLA leave. The leave may be taken intermittently unless it is for birth or adoption of a child, in which then the leave must be taken continuously.

Employees are required to provide 30 days notice of the need to take leave if the need is foreseeable. If the need isn't foreseeable, notice must be provided as soon as possible. The employer is required to maintain your health benefits while you are out on leave. Further, when you come back from leave, you must be restored to at least the same level position unless certain exceptions are met.[14] Finally, the employer may not retaliate against an employee for exercising their rights under FMLA. As defenses, employers may argue that FMLA doesn't apply on either the employer or the employee side. In other words, if the employer doesn't have 50 or more employees or the employee hasn't worked at the company for long enough. Employers may also argue that the substantive provisions of FMLA haven't been met, meaning that either the medical condition is not a serious medical condition or

---

[14] For example, for highly compensated employees, if reinstatement would lead to "substantial" and "grievous" problems for employer, then the employer need not reinstate the employee.

that the leave isn't for providing care to an ill family member (i.e. it's for vacation).

As mentioned above, some states have their own FMLA and require paid leave.[15] These state laws also have requirements for which employees and which employers are subject to the laws. Many are the same as the federal FMLA. For example, California requires employers with five or more employees to provide 12 weeks of paid leave to employees who have worked at least 1,250 hours for the employer within the past year. The California law also explicitly covers bonding with a child who becomes part of the family through foster care.

F. Wellness Programs

Believe it or not, there are a significant amount of regulations surrounding wellness programs offered by employers. What are wellness programs? They are programs offered by the employer to employees to improve and promote health and fitness, including programs to stop smoking, lose weight, or otherwise improve health metrics. Notably, in running these programs, employers may not discriminate against people with disabilities or significant conditions. Further, employers may have an implicit motivation for offering these wellness programs because the healthier their employees are, the less money the employer must spend on health insurance.

There are two types of wellness programs: participatory and health contingent. Under a participatory program, the employee receives some kind of incentive simply for participating. For a health contingency program, the incentive is awarded only when the

[15] As of January 1, 2024, the following state have paid family leave laws: California, Colorado, Connecticut, D.C., Maryland, Massachusetts, New Jersey, New York, Oregon, Rhode Island, and Washington. The Department of Labor gathers state law information here: https://www.dol.gov/agencies/whd/state/fmla.

employee has achieved a health goal. Under the ACA, the incentives are subject to caps: employers may offer up to 30% of the heath premium and up to 50% of the premium for a tobacco cessation wellness program. However, at all times, the employer must prove there is not a pretext for discrimination based on health status and for a health contingency plan, the employer must offer an alternative to obtain the incentive for employees who are unable to complete the program.

For programs that contain biometric screening or health risk assessment, the Americans with Disabilities Act and Genetic Information Nondisclosure Act require that participation be voluntary. Further, the EEOC issued proposed rules that such programs must only offer minimum incentives (like a coffee mug). However, these regulations were withdrawn, and new regulations have not yet been proposed.

G. Pregnancy Benefits

As discussed in Chapter 4, the Pregnancy Discrimination Act ("PDA") prohibits employers from discriminating on the basis of pregnancy, childbirth or related medical conditions, and requires covered employers to treat women "affected by pregnancy, childbirth or related medical conditions" the same as employees "not so affected."[16] Congress enacted the PDA after a pair of Supreme Court cases holding that it was not a violation of Title VII or the Equal Protection Clause to exclude pregnancy from disability benefits.[17]

More recently, Congress enacted the Pregnant Workers Fairness Act ("PWFA").[18] The PWFA only applies to accommodations

---

[16] 42 U.S.C. § 2000e(k).

[17] Gilbert v. General Electric, 429 U.S. 125 (1976); Geduldig v. Aiello, 417 U.S. 484 (1974).

[18] 42 U.S.C. § 2000gg.

and does not replace laws that are more protective of pregnant workers. Covered employers are private and public sector employers with at least 15 employees, Congress, federal agencies, employment agencies, and labor organizations. Under the PWFA, employers must provide reasonable accommodations to a pregnant employee or applicant for known limitations related to pregnancy, childbirth or related medical conditions unless doing would lead to an undue hardship for the employer. "Undue hardship" is defined as significant difficulty or expense.

What type of accommodations might an employer provide? Well, imagine you are pregnant at work—what might you need to continue your employment? How about uniforms and safety apparel that fits properly, light duty assignments, additional break time to use the bathroom (trust me, this is key), the ability to sit while working, and perhaps closer parking.

In additional to requiring the provision of accommodations, covered employers are prohibited from requiring a covered employee to accept an accommodation other than any reasonable accommodation arrived at through the interactive process or to take leave, whether paid or unpaid, if another reasonable accommodation can be provided. Employers also may not deny employment opportunities to a qualified employee if such denial is based on the need to make reasonable accommodations or take adverse action in terms, conditions, or privileges of employment against a qualified employee on account of the employee requesting or using a reasonable accommodation.

Finally, as with all anti-discrimination statutes, employers are prohibited from retaliating against an employee for exercising their rights under the statute.

> **TIP:** If an employee is not hired or fired simply because she is pregnant, that is a PDA issue. If the employee is denied a light duty assignment because she is pregnant

and has been advised by a medical professional that she needs such an assignment, that is a PWF issue.

IN SUMMARY: To understand the intricate landscape of healthcare and employer benefits, you must consider the various federal statutes and private employer benefits separately. Federal statutes like ERISA, ADA, and FMLA outline both the employer and employee obligations owed to one another in order to reap the benefits and coverage of the laws. In your studies of Employment Law, keep in mind the various legal frameworks and obligations and always ask "who is covered?" under the various statutes. Additionally, pay close attention to any exceptions or carve-outs in the statutes.

CHAPTER 7

Workplace Safety and Compensation

Workers get injured at work in big ways and small. In shocking news to no one who has read the first six chapters of this book, multiple state and federal laws deal with workplace safety. In this chapter, we will focus on the laws that try to prevent workplace injuries and then the laws that compensate workers who do suffer injuries.

A. Workplace Safety

Let's start with the most expansive federal law—the Occupational Safety and Health Act ("OSHA") of 1970.[1] OSHA covers 130 million workers and over 8 million workplaces in every state, D.C., and Puerto Rico. OSHA preempts all state laws unless the state has an approved plan.[2] The goal of OSHA is to prevent injuries and deaths. The Act operates on the premise that employers are following the regulations promulgated by the Department of Labor and those regulations are enforced through inspections. Unlike

[1] 29 U.S.C. §§ 651-678.

[2] To be an approved plan, the state plan must be at least as effective as OSHA, must require identical reports, and must cover state and local government employees.

many other statutes, there is no right of action for employees to sue for violations of OSHA.

1. *Definition of Employer*

Given the above statistic, you might have an inkling that the definition of "employer" under OSHA is broad. You would be correct! OSHA applies to employers and is unhelpfully defined as "persons engaged in business affecting commerce who have employees," not including the United States or a state.[3] Also excluded from OSHA purview are workplaces over which other federal agencies have jurisdiction and have chosen to regulate.[4] For workplaces which fall within the "affecting commerce" definition, courts have described the burden of demonstrating that the business affects commerce as a "modest" one, requiring "substantial" evidence of the affect on commerce that reasonable minds would accept as adequate.[5]

2. *Basics—Promulgating Standards*

OSHA is administered by the Department of Labor. The Secretary of Labor has two areas of obligations under OSHA: promulgation of safety standards and inspections to enforce those standards, accompanied by the issuance of citations for violations. Standards promulgated under OSHA must regulate working conditions. In other words, the hazards at issue must be occupational and the injuries to be avoided must be work-related. Further, these hazards must be located in the workplace itself.[6]

---

[3] 29 U.S.C. § 652(5).

[4] There are other exclusions, such as farms that employ only immediate family members.

[5] See, e.g. Chao v. OSHRC, 401 F.3d 355 (2005).

[6] Applying this test, courts have found that housing for seasonal workers is part of the "workplace." Frank Diehl Farms v. Secretary of Labor, 696 F.2d 1325 (11th Cir. 1983).

To promulgate a new standard or to modify or revoke an existing standard, the Secretary must make certain findings under OSHA Section 6(b).[7] Procedurally, the Secretary must publish the proposed new standard in the Federal Register under the full notice and comment process for rulemaking. This is really difficult and takes YEARS to get a standard passed. As for the substantive requirements to pass a standard, the Secretary must prove that a standard is reasonably necessary OR appropriate to provide safe or healthful environment. This means that there has to be a significant risk of harm in the workplace which can be eliminated or lessened by a change in practices.[8]

Another method to promulgate a new standard is under OSHA Section 6(c) which allows Emergency Temporary Standards ("ETS"). These standards are intended to cover situations where there is grave danger from exposure to substances or agents known to be toxic. Courts have concluded that "grave danger" means life threatening. An ETS does not require full notice and comment, but the Secretary of Labor must begin the process to create a regular standard on same hazard within six months. If you have heard of an ETS standard recently, it is most likely because this is the method by which the Biden Administration sought to require employers to require COVID-19 vaccinations. As with most ETS standards, the Court blocked the ETS from going into effect.[9] There are only four instances of an ETS actually going into effect.

---

[7] For the first two years of OSHA's existence, the Secretary was able to establish standards without the formal rulemaking process. But that option, along with too much eyeliner and bad perms, is long gone.

[8] Indus. Union Dept. v. Amer. Petroleum Inst., 448 U.S. 607 (1980) (the Benzene case).

[9] Nat'l Fed'n of Indep. Bus., et al v. Dep't of Lab., Occupational Safety and Health Admin., 595 U.S. 109 (2022).

3. *Employer's Obligations*

Employers are required to meet what is known as the **general duty clause** as well as any specific standards relevant to its workplace. Further, they must also report injuries and maintain records. The general duty clause, found in OSHA Section 5(a)(1), requires employers to keep the workplace free from recognized hazards that are causing or likely to cause death or serious physical harm. This clause comes into play when there is not an applicable standard for the hazard at issue (like working with killer whales—see below).

In order to prove a violation of the general duty clause, the Secretary must prove:

1. the activity presented a hazard to employee;
2. either the employer or the industry recognized the activity as a hazard;
3. the hazard was likely to or actually caused death or serious physical harm; and
    - Keep in mind for this element that it doesn't mean the likelihood of the injury actually happening. It means if the employees come into contact with the hazard, what's the likelihood of its causing death or harm. In other words, it is not asking the likelihood of a bear attack at a law school but if there is a bear attack, what's the likelihood of death or serious harm.
4. a feasible means to eliminate or materially reduce the hazard existed.
    - Under this element, the court considers whether the means to reduce the hazard is economically and technologically capable of

being done. Further, these means must actually reduce the hazard. Proving that something is feasible isn't enough if that measure wouldn't add to the safety of the workplace.

In a popular case commonly included in casebooks, the court considered the general duty clause when an employee was drowned by a killer whale.[10] The court found that working in close contact with killer whales was a "recognized hazard" and that abatement procedures to protect employees was feasible. Because SeaWorld did not protect its employees, the court held it had violated the general duty clause.

In addition, employers must comply with **specific standards.** These standards are incredibly detailed and are divided into four main categories: general industry, construction, maritime and longshoring, and agriculture. General industry is basically all businesses that don't fall into the other categories. Within these categories, many, many, many workplace safety issues are covered. Just to pick one example, there are OSHA regulations on whether a worker could bring their coffee maker from home to the workplace!

In order to prove a violation of a **specific standard**, OSHA must prove:

1. the applicability of standard;
    - This can involve complicated questions as to whether a specific industry falls within one of the four groupings.
2. the existence of a violation;
3. employee exposure to the violation; and

[10] SeaWorld of Florida, LLC v. Perez, 748 F.3d 1202 (D.D.C. 2014)

4. the employer knew or should have known of violation.

4. *Enforcement*

With all of these standards that employers must meet, how is OSHA actually enforced? It all begins with compliance officers coming to a workplace and inspecting the workplace. That said, there are so few compliance officers that the chance of being inspected is incredibly low. Still, there are two types of inspections—**programmed** (which take place according to set standards) and **unprogrammed** (which take pace after a fatality or a complaint). Employers may require the inspection officer to obtain an inspection warrant.[11] Everything about the inspection must be reasonable—the time of the inspection, the manner of the inspection, and the scope of the inspection. Further, if the inspection is happening due to a complaint about a specific issue, then the inspection is limited to that issue. After the inspection, the officer then issues a report.

Now the real fun begins. The Area Director determines whether to issue a citation for any violations. The citation must be in writing, must describe the violation, set a reasonable time to fix the violation, and list the proposed penalties. This must be issued within six months of the inspection. Then, the employer has to post the citation at the workplace. There are several categories of violations:

- De minimis
- Nonserious
- Serious
- Repeated

---

[11] Marshall v. Barlow's, Inc., 436 U.S. 307 (1978).

- Willful
- Failure to abate
- Failure to post

Most of the time, someone contests the citation or contests the category of the violation (i.e., serious v. nonserious). The employer, an employee, and the union (if there is one) have the right to contest the citation within 15 days of the issuance. If the citation isn't contested, it becomes final and is not reviewable. If the citation is contested, then a whole process is set into motion.

The notice of contest is sent to the Occupational Safety and Health Review Commission ("Commission"). Then there is a hearing before an administrative law judge.[12] The administrative law judge reaches a decision and send the decision to the Commission. But wait! There's more. The "aggrieved party" (aka the losing party) may request a petition for discretionary review. Any member of Commission may direct review of the decision. The Commission then reviews the decision and reaches its own decision. The aggrieved party from that decision may seek review of the final order of the Commission in the Court of Appeals for the circuit in which the violation occurred or the D.C. Circuit.

5. Employees' Rights

Despite not having the right to sue to enforce OSHA, employees do have a number of rights available under the statute. First, they have the right to refuse to perform a hazardous job activity if they reasonably believe there is a real danger of death or serious injury (but not just because its unsafe—has to be death or serious injury) and there is no time to resort to administrative action to remedy

---

[12] Note to law students—don't forget about administrative law judges when you are considering clerking!

the danger. However, if an employee acts in bad faith, then they can be fired for refusing to perform the job.

Further, employees have the right to petition for standards and to be informed of the standards for their workplace. They also have the right to request an inspection and then to assist the inspector. Employees are protected from retaliation for filing a complaint, testifying, or informally offering information. Employees also must comply with OSHA standards but can't be sanctioned by the Department of Labor if they don't. (They can be fired, of course). Finally, employees have the right to seek access to their own heath records held by the employer.

6. *Employer Defenses*

Employers have many different defenses at their disposal. Some are procedural, relating to the inspection itself and the timing of any citations issued. Other defenses focus on the substance of any violations found. For example, employers may contest the elements of the violation, or they may request a variance from the standard that is the subject of the violation.

There are also affirmative defenses available. The first is the **unpreventable or unavoidable employee misconduct**. As a litigator friend of mine once said, sometimes the last thing an employee says in these cases before the injury is "watch this!" The idea behind this defense is if the employer does everything reasonable to train, supervise, and prevent injuries and employees engage in dangerous nonsense, then employer should not be liable. The success of this defense will turn on the training and supervision provided by the employer. The second affirmative defense is **infeasibility**. Under this defense, the employer must prove that compliance is not possible, either technologically or economically by showing that they tried the alternative or there is no alternative. The third affirmative defense is a **"greater hazard"** defense. Here the employer must show that complying with the relevant standard would lead to a greater threat to employee health and safety.

7. *The Paperwork*

Oh, the paperwork. OSHA has many requirements for record keeping. For employers with over 11 employees, employers must keep records of occupational illnesses and injuries. Employers with fewer than 20 employees and in low hazard occupations are excused from much of the record keeping requirements but not the requirement that they report job related fatalities and multiple hospitalizations. Failure to keep records or report accurately is very serious. Employers who fail to do so face penalties.

There are very specific formats for record keeping and serious penalties for failure to maintain the records as required.[13] Once a year, the records must be sent to the agency and currently they must be sent electronically. The report forms must be kept for five years.

Further, in addition to keeping track of injuries and fatalities, employers must keep track of exposure to harmful or toxic materials that are regulated by a measuring or monitoring standard. Exposure records must be maintained for 30 years.

> **IN SUMMARY:** OSHA is premised on the idea that employers will meet the safety standards set forth in the regulations pre-inspection. The threat of inspections and fines is the back up to keep employers in compliance. OSHA has very specific regulations by industry with the general duty clause as the catchall provision. Employees cannot bring a private action to enforce OSHA but do have the right to ask for an inspection.

[13] Reading these requirements is very reminiscent to Office Space (the movie). Employers must file the OSHA 300, OSHA 300A, and the OSHA 301 reports.

B. Workers' Compensation

Now, imagine that despite OSHA, you are injured while at work. You would probably want to know the following questions: Can I get money? How? How much? How fast? For how long?

Our legal system has attempted to answer most of these questions through the workers' compensation system. The system provides the "exclusive" remedy for workplace injuries.[14] Prior to the creation of this system, workers injured on the job would sue their employers in tort with all the ensuing complications and unknowns. The idea is that both the employer and the injured employee gain and lose under this system. The workers' compensation system provides a benefit to employees with certain guaranteed benefits, but the employee gives up potentially higher paying tort claims. The employer benefits by not facing uncertain tort awards but gives up certain tort-based defenses (such as assumption of the risk). This is why you may read cases where the employer is arguing for workers' compensation to apply so it can avoid a potentially more costly tort claim.

1. So How Does This Work?

It's an insurance plan on a state level (the only federal component of workers' compensation is that federal workers and certain industries are exempted by federal statute because those workers are covered under other statutes).[15] Employers must either have insurance or self-insure.[16] For covered employees (see below) with covered injuries (see below), the system provides medical care, cash benefits, and rehabilitation services. The wage

[14] Intentional injuries caused by the employer do not fall within the workers' compensation system.

[15] For example, railroad employees, harbor workers, seamen, federal employees, and nuclear weapons industry employees are covered under other federal statutes.

[16] Except for Texas, where it is elective.

replacement varies dependent on the severity and duration of the injury.

2. Which Employers Count as Covered Employers?

As with much of employment law, this is dependent on state law. However, in most states, holding workers' compensation insurance is mandatory for most employers and the definition of employer is very broad. To use Pennsylvania as an example, "employer" is defined as an employer that employs at least one worker who could be injured or develop a work-related disease in the state or in some way connected with the state.[17]

3. Which Workers Count as Covered Employees?

Again, here coverage is very broad and typically begins on the first day of employment. "Employee" is often defined in such sweeping terms as "all natural persons who perform services for another for a valuable consideration." Of more interest are the exemptions that exist under workers' compensation statutes. As noted above, federal workers covered by another statute are exempt. However, many states exempt domestic workers or seasonal agricultural workers who earn less than a set amount during the year. Connecticut exempts professional athletes for example. Finally, some states provide an exemption due to religious beliefs.

4. What Injuries Are Covered?

Workers' compensation statutes are written and interpreted in favor of broad coverage. Physical injuries and mental injuries connected with a physical injury are covered. To be covered,

---

[17] For example, an employee could be based in Pennsylvania but injured outside of the state while on a work assignment.

injuries and occupational diseases must have occurred in the course of employment and arising out of employment. An occupational disease is a disease that is peculiar to the employee's occupation.

5. *What Counts as "In the Course of Employment"?*

Think of the test as a time, place, and circumstances test.

- Did the injury occur on the premises?
- Did it occur during working hours?
- Was the employee engaging in an activity the employer requested?
- Did the employer provide training to perform the activity?
- Did the activity benefit the employer?

As a general rule, if the employee's actions are a good faith effort to advance the interest of employer, the injury will be covered. (Remember, broad coverage is the intent!).

Often workers' compensation cases involve a one-time injury in mind (e.g., a fall from a ladder or a machine malfunctioning); however, gradual or repeated trauma injuries may be covered as well. Such injuries can raise questions of the date of the injury. For example, when did the carpal tunnel start? Courts will look to factors such as the date the injury manifested itself, the last exposure to injury causing device, and the last day the employee worked.

If an injury is compensable (if everything above is met), there is still another limitation. The injury must prevent the employee from working for a certain number of days. In other words, if you need one day off, you won't be covered by workers' compensation.

The minimum number of days ranges from three to seven, dependent on state law.

Let's consider some common questions. **Is an employee covered for injuries that occur when the employee is at work but engaged in some sort of personal activity?** For instance, eating lunch, or stretching in the break room. These activities are still considered to be in the course of employment. Well, you say, what if I'm injured during the company softball game? (Far more common than you might think). Injuries that occur during a recreational or social event may be covered if it is a benefit to the employer and the employee is expected to participate such that the event becomes part of the job. If your coworkers are goofing off and shoving each other and you get knocked over and injured, that is also a compensable injury.

Speaking of goofing off, many states will find an injury outside the scope of employment if the employee was injured because they violated a safety rule. For the injury to be found not compensable, the employer must show:

1. the employer expressly and specifically informed the employee not to perform the specific task;
2. the employee knew and understood the restriction;
3. the employer did not knowingly accept the benefit of a violation; and
4. the injury occurred because the employee violated the rule.

6. Arising out of Employment.

To be compensable, an injury must also **"arise out of employment."** Generally, this means the injury's origin must be in an employment related risk. Imagine an injury that occurs while an employee is walking home from a bar to the hotel while on an out-of-town job assignment and is hit by a car. Those injuries would not be covered. Although travelling may be part of the job and therefore in the course of employment, the injury didn't arise out of that employment. But being stuck with a needle while taking out of the trash (when taking out the trash is part of the job) would be compensable. There is interesting ongoing litigation over whether a teacher who was shot by a student is limited to workers' compensation (as opposed to a $40 million tort claim). Is being shot by a student an injury arising out of employment for teachers? Stay tuned.[18]

What about injuries that occur while commuting? In other words, if you fall asleep driving home from a late shift and are injured in a car accident, are those injuries covered? The answer is no. Those injuries are not within the course of employment and do not arise out of employment. The only exception for commuting is when the injuries occur on employer provided transportation.

What about working from home? With so many more people working remotely these days, are any injuries covered if the injury occurs at home? Just because the employee is working from home does not automatically remove workers' compensation coverage. But all the above criteria still apply to injuries that occur while working from home. The injury must be within the scope of employment and arising out of employment. In fact, some states have a rebuttable presumption that if an employee is killed or unable to testify due to the injury, that injury is presumed to arise out of and in the course of employment, even if the employee was working from home.

There is a surprising amount of case law dealing with employees being struck by lightning while working. Some states look to see if the employment task exposed the employee to the

---

[18] The case is Zwerner v. Newport News School District and is in Virigina state court.

particular danger that brought about the injury. In other words, did the job expose the employee to the lightning strike? The employee needs to be subject to a risk which members of the general public are not equally exposed in order to be covered by workers' compensation. For example, a police officer interviewing a suspect outside on a porch during a storm was not subject to a different risk than members of the general public.

Does workers' compensation apply to pre-existing conditions? For example, if an employee has a heart condition because of years of smoking and then has a heart attack at work while lifting heavy items, does workers' compensation cover those injuries? Maybe! Such an injury may be covered if:

1. the employment contributed to the injury in a significant manner;
2. work stress accelerated the injury; and
3. there are no intervening causes (such as the employee's own negligence).

7. If All of the Above Is Shown, How Does the Employee Actually Get the Compensation?

The basic procedure is as follows. The employee informs the employer of the injury. The employer then makes a report to the relevant state agency. The employee files a claim for the workers' compensation benefits. The employer may dispute that claim as failing to meet some part of the above requirements. If so, the state agency will investigate and there may be a hearing by an administrative law judge. And if that decision is then contested, there can be an appeal to the state workers compensation Commission.

8. *What Are the Benefits?*

First, keep in mind that employees are covered by workers' compensation on the first day of work. There is no "after you have worked for so many hours" requirement. Injured employees will need to provide proof of the injury and the limitations on work from a medical professional. Under many state systems, employers have a limited time to contest whether an injury is work-related (e.g., 21 days).

The benefits fall into three categories: wage replacement, medical benefits, and death benefits. A very common level of wage replacement is 2/3 of the statewide average weekly wage. Medical benefits include things such as physician services, hospital and surgical care, nursing care, medications, medical supplies, appliances, and prosthetic devices. What does "appliance" mean in this context? A necessary appliance could be a laptop so that the employee can continue to work from home, or an appliance could include a wheelchair accessible van to make a wheelchair fully useful. Death benefits are awarded to survivors of workers who die from work related injuries based on the workers earnings and the number of dependents.

There are several benefit levels:

- Temporary Total Disability: the employee is temporarily prevented from performing the job.
- Temporary Partial Disability: benefits paid during a period of reduced earnings; the benefits stop when the worker returns to full wages or is eligible for permanent total disability.
- Permanent Total Disability: if a worker hits the maximum medical improvement and these serious impairment remains that causes disability for an indefinite period of time.

- Permanent Partial Disability: there are permanent impairments that do not completely limit the ability to work.

One final thing to keep in mind, most state workers' compensation statutes protect against retaliation for making a workers' compensation claim.[19]

IN SUMMARY: Workers' compensation systems are based in state law and act to provide set benefits to injured workers and protect employers from large tort judgments. To recover, an injured worker must have sustained the injury in course of employment and arising out of employment. Employees who are injured as a result of violating a reasonable employer safety rule will be excluded from coverage.

[19] At least one court found that the anti-retaliation provisions of the state law at issue did not protect applicants for employment.

CHAPTER 8

Employee Liberty

Overall, employees believe they have more rights at work than they actually do. Remember the employment-at-will adage: the employer can fire you for a good reason, a bad reason, or no reason at all. Taken to the extreme, this means the employer could fire you for skiing on the weekend or because of what you say or wear at work. What about the mode of transportation you use to get to work? (This actually happened during the pandemic!)

Some states have sought to protect employees by enacting legislation ("lifestyle laws") that prohibit employers from taking action against employees for legal activities taken off-work site.[1] For example, New York prevents an employer from taking adverse action against an employee for the employee's legal political activities, legal recreational activities, and legal use of consumable products. But if the employee's activities create a conflict of interest with the employer's business, then the employer may take action to protect legitimate employer interests. Similar to New York's protection of "legal consumables," although employers may ban smoking or vaping in the workplace, states have explicitly

1 California, Colorado, New York, and North Dakota have "lifestyle" laws.

prohibited employers from taking action against employees for smoking outside of the job.

Apart from state specific "lifestyle" statutes, there are other, broader categories of behavior that fall under the category of "employee liberty." In this chapter, we will focus on speech, dress and grooming, and privacy. To determine the protections for employees in these areas, you must consider the following questions:

- What type of employer? (public or private)
- What is the job at issue?
- What is the restriction the employer is imposing?
- What is the source of the right?
- Is there a union or collective bargaining agreement ("CBA") to consider?

A. Speech

When considering employee speech rights, it's very important to distinguish whether you are dealing with public or private employment. Very. VERY. What counts as speech? In addition to actual verbal conversations in the workplace, published writings (think of blog posts) also count as speech. This can include actions such as liking, reposting, and commenting on social media.

1. Public Sector

Let's begin with protections for speech for public (governmental) employees. There is no right to public employment (see Chapter 9 for more on this) but once employed by a public entity, an employee may not be fired for exercising a constitutional right. Governments acting as employers have more latitude than when they act as a sovereign. However, there are still some restrictions. The restrictions on employer actions in the realm of speech is found in the First Amendment. To successfully claim protection under the First Amendment, the employee must prove that the action was constitutionally protected and was a substantial or motivating factor in the employer's action against them.

Speech of Public Concern. The threshold question turns on the content of the speech. Speech unrelated to the workplace is pure citizen speech and can't be restricted by the government. If the speech is related to the workplace, then the court must decide if the speech was a matter of public concern.[2]

Of course, there is no bright line test for what speech counts as a "matter of public concern." Consider this: an employee in a Sheriff's Office, when discussing the assassination attempt on President Reagan says to another employee, "I hope they get him next time." Is that a matter of public concern? The Supreme Court said yes, because it was a comment on President Reagan's overall policies and therefore entitled to protection.[3]

However, in *Garcetti v. Ceballos*, 547 U.S. 410 (2006), the Court created an exception. When a public employee speaks within the context of his official duties (as opposed to as a private citizen), there is no constitutional protection for the speech. In *Garcetti*, a deputy District Attorney wrote a memo outlining problems with an affidavit used to obtain a search warrant and recommended a dismissal of the charges. He also gave testimony at trial. The Court found that because his job duties included reviewing and discussing search warrants, the speech at issue was part of his official duties and therefore not a matter of public concern.

---

2 Connick v. Myers, 461 U.S. 138 (1983).

3 Rankin v. McPherson, 483 U.S. 378 (1987).

Because this analysis can turn on what exactly an employee's job duties are, this should be a reminder that every public employer should have a solid job responsibilities chart for every employee!

***Pickering* balancing.** Determining that the speech at issue is a matter of public concern is only the first step. Next, a balancing step must be applied. The Court developed this test in *Pickering v. Board of Education*, 391 U.S. 563 (1968). In this case, a public school teacher sent a letter to the local paper about the school board's spending, specifically the allocation of funds between academics and athletics. Some of the statements were false. The school board terminated the teacher's employment after he sent the letter. The Court described the analysis as requiring "balancing the interests of the [employee], as a citizen, in commenting on matters of public concern and the interest of the State, as an employer, in promoting efficiency of the public services it performs through its employees."[4]

You will not be surprised to hear that there is no set test for the employer's interest. Courts look to issues such as harmony among co-workers, maintaining discipline by immediate supervisors, performance of employee's duties, and the operation of the office.

> **IN SUMMARY:** Imagine a public employee writes a blog post touching on the workplace and is later disciplined. Is this speech protected? First, you must consider the content of the speech: is it on a matter of public concern or is just venting about the office? If it is a matter of public concern, is it within the official duties of the employee? Will this blog post cause problems for the employee in the performance of their job of the ability of the supervisors to keep the efficient operation of the

---

[4] Pickering v. Bd. of Educ., 391 U.S. 563, 568 (1968).

office going? Only after answering these fact specific questions will it be clear whether the speech is protected.

2. *Private Sector*

It is a much tougher road for private sector employees to bring a claim based on speech. Because constitutional protections do not apply to the private sector, employees who believe they have been disciplined due to their speech need to look to other avenues. Some states provide a state based statutory or constitutional right to freedom of speech. In those cases, the employee needs to rely on the contours of the state law to determine if they have a claim.

Another option is to consider the anti-discrimination statutes. For example, if a member of a protected class believes they are disciplined more severely than other employees, there could be an anti-discrimination claim. Or if the speech at issue could be considered protected activity under the statute (opposing some unlawful action), the employee may have a retaliation claim. Importantly, for the anti-retaliation provisions to apply, the speech must be opposing an alleged unlawful practice or must count as "participation" under the statute (see Chapter 4 for a discussion of retaliation claims).

The National Labor Relations Act ("NLRA") protects employees who are engaged in "concerted activity." Although you may think that the NLRA only covers workers who are union members, the concerted activity provision applies to all workers. So, if an employee emails all their co-workers to join in a challenge to a new policy in the workplace, the NLRA would protect the employee for that action.

There is also the possibility of a claim for a violation of public policy. However, the speech itself would have to be considered part of public policy or the subject of the speech would need to be considered a matter of public policy.

In short, absent a state statute providing private sector employees with speech protection, a private sector employee is vulnerable to discipline for their speech.

B. Dress and Grooming

What you wear and how you present yourself may seem like something your employer should have no say in. However, employers are able to set standards for the workplace that cover everything from clothes to hair length, facial hair, makeup, jewelry, and body art. But this ability is not without limits!

Public employees have fought against these kind of restrictions with freedom of expression claims, equal protection claims, and 14th Amendment due process claims based on a liberty interest in personal appearance. In practice, courts have been deferential to governments acting as employers in this area, particularly when the job at issue is law enforcement. In *Kelley v. Johnson*, 425 U.S. 238 (1976), the Supreme Court upheld a police department's restriction on hair length and facial hair. The Court assumed a liberty interest in personal appearance existed but found that the governmental as employer is entitled to deference in its internal affairs which includes "choice of organization." The employees challenging the restriction would need to demonstrate there is no rational connection between the regulation and the promotion of safety of persons and property.

Private employees, again, do not have the same rights as public employees and have turned to state laws and to anti-discrimination laws. A common conflict between employee's dress and an employer's policy is in the area of religious beliefs. Some employee's religious beliefs may require them to wear modest or loose-fitting clothes, headwear of some kind, or to display some outward symbol of their beliefs. Recall from Chapter 4 that employers are required to provide accommodations for an employee's religious beliefs and practices unless doing so would create an undue hardship.[5]

The employee must show that their sincere religious belief conflicts with an employment requirement. However, the Supreme Court made clear there is no requirement that the employer actually know that there is a conflict between an applicant's religious practice and a work rule.[6] This may sound confusing but the Court was drawing a distinction between knowledge and intent. In other words, if the employer believes it may have to provide such an accommodation due to a religious belief and is motivated by the desire to avoid having to accommodate a religious practice, failure to hire the potential employee is a violation of Title VII.

Further, although the first step in these claims is to show the employee's sincere religious belief, courts are very opposed to delving into a person's sincere religious belief. Typically, courts will accept the employee's statement of the sincere religious belief. For example, in *Cloutier v. Costco Wholesale Corp.*, 390 F.3d 126 (1st Cir. 2004), the court assumed the plaintiff's stated beliefs of the Church of Body Modification constituted a religious belief and moved on to determine whether a reasonable accommodation had been offered to her belief that she needed to always display her piercings. (FYI—apart from any religious claims, employers are able to require employees to cover their tattoos while at work or even to refuse to hire anyone with a tattoo.)

In the area of sex discrimination in grooming and dress codes, as mentioned in Chapter 4, employees have challenged employer dress codes when the dress code imposes an unequal burden on one sex over the other or is premised upon stereotypes. For example, in *Jesperson v. Harrah's Operating Co.*, 444 F.3d 1104 (9th Cir. Apr.

---

[5] Also recall that the new definition of "undue hardship" for religious accommodations is a substantial burden on the employer's business.

[6] EEOC v. Abercrombie & Fitch Stores, 575 U.S. 768 (2015).

14, 2006), the plaintiff argued that the make-up requirement for female employees required her to spend more time and money than male employees. Although the plaintiff lost (she didn't have evidence as to the burden), the court accepted the concept of the unequal burden as a viable challenge.

In addition to claims under anti-discrimination statutes, employer actions taken on the basis of hairstyle may run afoul of legislation known as the CROWN Act (Create a Respectful and Open World for Natural Hair). This legislation prohibits adverse action in employment (and education) based on natural hair texture and protective hair styles. As of this writing, 23 states and multiple municipalities have enacted legislation inspired by the CROWN Act.[7]

C. Privacy

"Privacy" encompasses a myriad of issues but they all revolve around the employer obtaining information about applicants and employees. The information could be a background check prior to employment, or it could be reading employee emails. Prior to employment, an employer may perform a background check, criminal record check, credit check, or search social media.[8] Questions arise both from how an employer gathers information but also what the employer does with that information.

Employers have always surveilled their employees and surveillance has only increased as technology has grown and improved. Imagine you have discovered that your employer is spying on you; perhaps videoing you in the workplace. Most states provide a tort claim for invasion of privacy, although the exact contours of

---

[7] The U.S. House of Representatives passed a CROWN Act in 2022 but the legislation did not pass in the Senate.

[8] Every semester, to prove a point, I give one of my teenage daughters a few names of students in my Employment Law class and tell her to see what she can find online. She's scary.

the right will depend on state law. Sometimes this is known as the tort of intrusion. This tort has two elements:

1. The employer has intruded into place, conversation or matter as to which the plaintiff has a ***reasonable expectation of privacy***; and

2. The intrusion occurred in a manner ***highly offensive to a reasonable person***.

For this tort, it doesn't matter what the employer does with the information, the tort is the intrusion itself. Unfortunately, there is not a clear standard employed by the courts for what level of privacy employees may expect in the workplace (remember these are state law claims and thus dependent on the parameters of state law!). Expectations of privacy may depend on the place where the intrusion occurred—a public space, a cubicle, an office with a lock on the door. When considering whether the manner is highly offensive, courts consider the means of intrusion—a written questionnaire; questions from the supervisor in a face-to-face meeting; a hidden camera; wiretapping; a search of email. Each of these means could be highly offensive.

A case commonly used in casebooks is *K-Mart Corp. Store No. 7441 v. Trotti*, 677 S.W.2d 632 (Tex. App. 1984). In this case, the employer provided a locker to the employee, but the employer allowed the employee to purchase and place her own lock on the locker. She sued when her manager searched her belongings in the locker. The court noted that the employee had a reasonable expectation of privacy because she had purchased her own lock. If the employer had provided the lock, there may not have been an expectation of privacy.

Other privacy violations may occur if the employer uses an employee name or likeness for its own advantage (i.e., your picture is in promotional materials) without your permission. Disclosing information may itself be another type of intrusion if the disclosure is offensive to a reasonable person and it's not a matter of public concern. Employers may defend against these claims by showing that the disclosure or surveillance was necessary to business operations or occurred with the consent of the employee.

Keep in mind that an employer can defeat expectations of privacy by maintaining a policy that the use of employer issued devices may be monitored (this applies to public and private employer workplaces). Similarly, although the federal Stored Communications Act (18 U.S.C. §§ 2701-12) limits searches of communications stored electronically, there is an exception for employers when notice is given to workers that their computers and stored communications are subject to search.[9]

> **Note**: You should know that if your employer provides the device and lets you know that they will monitor it, then you have ZERO expectations of privacy (Hi Boss!).

D. Polygraphs

Polygraphs (i.e., lie detector tests)[10] are covered by a federal statute that prohibits private employers from using lie detector tests for applicants or current employees (but doesn't apply to paper and pencil tests).[11] It has a broad scope, applying to all employers "engaged in or affecting commerce or in the production of goods for commerce." Basically, employers can't require employees to take a lie detector test, ask about the results of such a test, or fire someone based on the results of the test.

---

[9] If the information is stored outside of the employer, then there is a violation of the statute.

[10] Did you know that person who invented one of the early prototypes of the lie detector is also the creator of Wonder Woman? It's true! Golden Lasso of Truth, indeed.

[11] Employee Polygraph Protection Act of 1988, 29 U.S.C. §§ 2001-2009.

There are a few exceptions—if the employer is investigating workplace misconduct with economic loss, the employer may require an employee to take a test after a host of other requirements are met but even then, the employee cannot be fired without further evidence. Security services may test applicants and employers involved in drug manufacturing may test applicants and employees in certain situations.

As mentioned, the federal statute doesn't apply to paper and pencil honesty tests; however, some state laws do prohibit those as well.

E. Genetic Information

As part of the Genetic Information Nondiscrimination Act ("GINA") (discussed in Chapter 4), employees cannot request or purchase information about employees or family members of an employee. Employers also cannot take adverse actions against employees based on genetic information. For example, firing an employee because the employee's family has the gene which predisposed one to breast cancer is a violation of GINA. The statute provides exceptions that pertain to meeting obligations under OSHA or the FMLA.

F. Privacy and Public Employees

As public employees, there are additional privacy protections, specifically the Fourth Amendment applies to anything that falls within a "search." For example, in *Ontario v. Quon*, 560 U.S. 746 (2010), a police department reviewed an officer's pager transcripts to determine the reason for the officer exceeding the monthly limit of messages. Spoiler alert—it was because he was sexting on the Department issued pager while on duty! Anyway . . . the Court held that the review constituted a search, the search was not unreasonable because the department redacted off duty messages and because it was a reasonable way to determine if the excess pages were work related.

Public employees may also a have an associational right that protects privacy interests. This right is grounded in the liberty interest in Due Process Clause of 14th Amendment and the First Amendment association rights. Under this right, the employer cannot require public sector employees to disclose their organizational memberships. There is a split as to whether the *Pickering* test (discussed above under the speech information) applies—in other words, does the association need to be an association centered on a matter of public concern?

G. Social Media

Many states have passed legislation prohibiting employers from requiring employees to release passwords to personal social media accounts or to add an employee to their account or to change privacy settings. There are exceptions for employer-issued devices and employer created accounts.

H. Drug and Alcohol Testing

The government, acting as employer, may require employees to submit to drug and alcohol testing but such testing is considered a search. As such, testing must be reasonable, and courts will balance the right of privacy against the government's interest in conducting the search.[12] The Americans with Disabilities Act ("ADA") addresses "medical inquiries." If the inquiry occurs prior to starting the job, an employer may inquire into the ability of an applicant to perform the job. The employer may condition an offer of employment on the results of a medical exam on two conditions:

---

[12] Skinner v. Ry. Lab. Exec.' Ass'n, 489 U.S. 602 (1989); Nat'l Treasury Emps. Union v. Von Raab, 489 U.S. 656 (1989).

all new employees must take the exam and the results are kept confidential.

The law is a little different for current employees. Employers are prohibited from requiring medical exams or inquiries of employees unless it is job related and business necessity. If the employer has a reasonable objective concern about the employee's ability to do the job, the employer can require a medical exam but, as with applicants, the results must be confidential.

However, keep in mind that testing for illegal drug use does not need to meet these requirements.

I. Masks and Vaccinations

Employee liberty issues were blasted all over the news during the COVID-19 pandemic. Employees questioned whether their employers could force them to wear a mask or to become vaccinated. In short, the answer is yes. As long as the employer provided an exemption for religious accommodations and medical accommodations under the ADA, the employer could require employees to wear a mask or become vaccinated. Similarly, employers could prohibit masks as long as the same exemptions are present.

> **IN SUMMARY:** Employees have fewer rights in the workplace than many expect. Government employees are able to bring challenges under the Constitution for Equal Protection and Due Process claims. Private sector employees may have statutory claims under the anti-discrimination statutes if relevant. Otherwise, employees may look to state tort law for claims of invasion of privacy. Many states have enacted statutes providing employees with protection from adverse employment action on a range of topics from smoking to natural

hairstyles to their social media accounts. As always, it is important to check state and local law!

CHAPTER 9

Security of Employment

"They can't fire me for that!" Actually . . . remember, at-will employees presumptively have no job security. They can be fired for any reason at all as long as it isn't a prohibited reason. However, as we will see in this Chapter, there are now many restrictions on the employer's ability to terminate employment. These restrictions come from many sources—statutory, constitutional, contract, and tort law.

A. Statutory Protections

1. Antidiscrimination Statutes

As is clear from Chapter 4, the anti-discrimination laws (both federal and state) place restrictions on employers' reasons to terminate employment. As a reminder, for a basis covered in an anti-discrimination statute such as race, religion, age, disability status, sex, veteran status, the employer cannot terminate employment on that basis. In other words, an employer may fire an employee who is Catholic because they are embezzling, but not because they are Catholic.

2. Whistleblower Statutes

There are many, many statutes protecting whistleblowers. Whistleblowers are employees who report internal misconduct to outside authorities. These statutes protect the whistleblower from adverse action due to the whistleblowing and therefore restrict the employer's ability to terminate the employment.

To bring a successful whistleblower claim, the terminated employee must prove the following three elements:

- They engaged in a protected activity;
- They suffered an adverse action; and
- There is a causal link between the activity and the adverse action.[1]

The first element often causes a problem for employees bringing claims. The activity at issue must fall within the protections of the statute. For example, if a statute protects employees who report on *financial wrongdoing* and an employee at a bank reports on a *workplace safety issue*, the employee will not have a claim under the whistleblower statute. And as always with these claims, the employee will have to prove that the whistleblowing activity is the reason for the termination as opposed to another reason, like habitual lateness.

3. State Good Cause Statutes

Although this subheading says, "State Good Cause Statutes," it should really read "Montana's Good Cause Statute." This is because Montana is the only state with a statute that requires employers to have good cause to terminate an employee (and yes, it only protects employees, not independent contractors).[2]

---

1 Bard v. Bath Iron Works Corp., 590 A.2d 152 (1991).

2 *See* Marcy v. Delta Airlines, 166 F.3d 1279 (9th Cir. 1999).

The statute defines "good cause" as a legitimate business reason and it must have logical relationship to the needs of the business. This seems fairly broad, right? The statute goes on to state that an employer's reason is not legitimate if it is invalid as a matter of law, rests on mistaken interpretation of law, or is not the real reason.

The Montana statute also protects employees from termination when the employer fails to follow express procedures in its own written policies and when an employee refuses to violate public policy.

4. *Lifestyle Statutes*

Finally, recall from Chapter 8 that many states have passed "lifestyle" laws that prohibit employers from terminating employment for employees' legal actions outside of the workplace and working hours. For example, you can't fire someone in Illinois because they are a smoker or fire someone in New York because they go skiing on the weekend.

B. Constitutional Protections

Public sector employers are limited by the Constitution. Anti-discrimination provisions such as the Equal Protection Clause will impose limits on the public sector employer as well as Due Process concerns. Additionally, there are procedural Due Process concerns. However, terminated public sector employees have a few substantive claims at their disposal. Generally, the substantive Due Process arguments fall along two lines—a **property interest** and a **liberty interest**.

For the **property interest** claim, public sector employees need to recognize that the property interest has to be protectable to create any obligation on the part of the employer. Public sector employment may still be at-will employment and those at-will employees have no protectable property interest in employment. To demonstrate a protectable interest, employees will need to look to state law (if a state employee) or an implied contract. However, the mere fact that there is a written document pertaining to employment does not mean there is a property interest. For example, a collective bargaining agreement which requires that the employer has a reason for terminating employment does not transform the at-will employment to a property interest. This determination is very fact specific and will turn on the state law and facts of the workplace.

The second type of claim is a deprivation of the employee's **liberty interest**. Public sectors employees have a liberty interest in their good name. This just means that individuals have the right to protect their reputation and good name from false accusations or harm. So, when the employer creates and disseminates a false and defamatory impression about the employee in connection with the employee's termination, the liberty interest requires the employer provide a name clearing hearing.[3] Imagine a municipality fires an employee after publicly announcing there was an embezzling problem in its office. Then, the municipality would need to provide a chance for that employee to clear their name.

C. Contract Law Restrictions

Contract law limits employers' ability to terminate employees willy-nilly. Both **express** and **implied** contracts may be created to provide employees with some enforceable rights.

---

[3] *See* Goetz v. Windsor Sch. Dist., 698 F.2d 606 (2d Cir. 1983).

1. Express Contracts

Written employment contracts might restrict the employer in the reasons for terminating the contract and binding the employer to a certain duration of employment. To effectively accomplish either of those restrictions, the contract must indicate the parties' intention to enter into employment that is NOT at-will. Courts strictly construe employment contracts and put the burden on the employee to establish that the employer intended to create a just cause contracts (requiring that the employer has just cause to terminate the employee). If a written contract includes a duration of the employment (e.g., one year) but does not include grounds for termination, courts will often infer that any termination must be for good cause.

What constitutes "just cause" to terminate? The exact contours are dependent on state law. That said, employee misconduct is always just cause to terminate. The trickier question is whether an economic downturn constitutes just cause. For this reason, many express written contracts include language providing that employment may be terminated for an economic reason. As with employers, employees may be restricted to a just cause quit (some of the issues are discussed in the next chapter). Employees should keep in mind that ending employment early from a job that mandates a definite duration may subject them to pay damages owed to the employer (such as the costs of finding a replacement) unless they can be excused for nonperformance.

Employers may also restrict themselves through an oral employment contract. An explicit oral statement by the employer of job security will suffice. However, such statements must be clear and unequivocal to overcome presumption of employment-at-will (i.e., it must be more than the employer flattering an employee to keep them around). Of course, the employee must demonstrate the traditional contract law elements—promise made, enforceable promise, breach, and damages. In the case of oral contracts, some courts require that the employee must provide additional consideration beyond continued employment to clarify the intent of the parties. Another often litigated issue is the question of what language creates a just cause restriction on the employer. Some courts have found language such as "acceptable sales performance" is not enough to create a just cause standard.[4] But other courts have found "meets sales targets" to restrict the reasons an employer may terminate employment.

One last issue for oral contracts, either express or implied, is the **Statute of Frauds** (remember your Contracts class?). The Statute of Frauds prohibits enforcement of a contract that cannot be completed within one year unless in writing. The success of this defense will often turn on the court's interpretation of the contract itself. Is it for employment for life or employment as long as the employee is alive? Courts have found that the defense does not defeat the contract because the employee might die within a year and therefore the contract may be completed within a year. Brutal.

2. *Implied Contracts*

Employers may create an implied promise to terminate only for good cause. These implied promises may be based upon oral statements, written documents, or the conduct of the parties.

The leading case (it's in all the casebooks!) for the implied promise for continued employment is *Pugh v. See's Candies*, 116 Cal. App. 3d 311 (1981). In that case, the employee worked for company for 32 years, rose through the ranks and then was terminated without explanation. (There was a cryptic comment that indicated it might be because he was challenging the pay for

---

[4] *See* Gordon v. Matthew Bender & Co., 562 F. Supp. 1286 (1983).

temporary workers.) The court found an implied in fact, just cause contract based on general factors such as:

- personnel practices of the industry;
- personnel policies of the employer;
- duration of employment, and;
- assurances of continued employment.

Specifically in *Pugh*, the court noted that the employee had worked for 32 years, received continued promotions, a lack of criticism of his work, and was told he would always have a job with the employer. Courts have since clarified that the duration of employment alone is not enough to create an implied just cause contract.

3. *Handbooks*

Perhaps the most common method by which employers restrict their ability to terminate employees is through a handbook or internal policies. Handbooks may state that employment will continue unless there is just cause for termination. Handbooks may also create a process for discipline, including termination, of employees. At times, courts look to statements in handbooks as support for oral statements made by the employer (i.e., the employer says, "just keep up the good work and you'll have a job" and the handbook provides procedures for termination).

For every handbook, the question is whether the employer has created an enforceable obligation through its handbook. Consider the usual requirements for a contract (offer, acceptance, bargained for consideration). Of these, "bargained for consideration" is the usual sticking point for handbooks creating an enforceable obligation on the employer. However, many courts have found that an employee's continued employment (they show up to work) when there is no contractual obligation to do so is enough to bind the employer to the promises made in the handbook.

So how does a court determine if a handbook is binding? Courts look to factors such as the timing of the receipt of the handbook by employees, which employees received the handbook, the acknowledgement of receipt of the handbook, steps taken to ensure that employees read the handbook, and even the title of the handbook (e.g., "Some Random Thoughts" v. "Office Policies and Procedures").

If an implied contract is created by a handbook, courts consider these contracts as **unilateral contracts.**[5] This raises questions as to an employer's ability to modify the handbook without providing any additional consideration to the employees. State law falls into three basic approaches. The first approach holds that because the handbook is a unilateral contract, the employer may withdraw or modify the handbook whenever it chooses (the offer), and employee accepts the new provisions by showing up to work the next day (the acceptance). A second approach holds that promises made in an old version of the handbook can't be unilaterally revoked (e.g., moving from a just cause standard to at-will employment) without a new offer, new acceptance, and additional consideration being offered. The third and more middle ground approach looks to the reasonableness of notice provided to employees of the changes and insists on *actual* notice of the changes.

Isn't this all solved by a disclaimer in the handbook? Basically, yes. If the employer includes language along the lines of "nothing in the handbook creates a binding obligation on the employer," the employer may have defeated any claim of binding obligations. However, the disclaimer must be clear, unambiguous, and

---

[5] *See* Woolley v. Hoffmann-La Roche, Inc., 499 A.2d 515 (1985).

prominent. Courts look for a separate section, different font, or larger print when deciding whether a disclaimer is proper.

4. *Promissory Estoppel*

Although not widely accepted, some workers have been successful with a claim of promissory estoppel. Once again, think back to your Contracts class. This doctrine seeks to enforce promises made when there is reasonable detrimental reliance even if there is no enforceable contract. The elements of a promissory estoppel claim are:

1. A promise;
2. A reasonable expectation to induce action or forbearance;
3. It does induce action or forbearance;
4. Injustice.

In the typical scenario that leads to a promissory estoppel claim, a worker is offered a new job, quits their old job, and then the new job offer is revoked. There is no contract and no assurances as to the duration of the new employment. However, that worker is now out of the old job and the new job! Those courts finding a promissory estoppel claim reason that the worker should be given a chance to perform the job duties.

Again, this is not universally accepted by courts and for those that do accept the doctrine, they limit its application by construing the reliance and promise elements narrowly. For a successful promissory estoppel claim, the worker receives reliance damages. These damages are intended to put the worker in the position they would have been in but for their reliance on the promise.

5. *Covenant of Good Faith and Fair Dealing*

The final contract law doctrine to consider is the covenant of good faith and fair dealing. Good faith and fair dealing obligates each party in a contract to refrain from injuring in any way the other's right to receive the benefits of the contract. As a matter of general contract law, this covenant is well accepted. However, It is far less accepted in employment law.

A minority of jurisdictions hold that the covenant of good faith and fair dealing applies to all contracts and applies to employment contracts with equal force. Therefore, the employer cannot take actions that would interfere with the rights of the employee to get the benefits of the contract. Another "in all the casebooks" case is *Fortune Cash Register v. NCR*, 373 Mass. 96 (1977). In *Fortune*, the employer terminates the employee after he has secured a large sale for the employer and before he would earn the bonus he was entitled to under the terms of his employment. The court held that depriving someone of compensation they earned is in bad faith and therefore a violation of the covenant. This interpretation of the covenant allows the employer to terminate employment but not in a way that deprives the employee of benefits already earned.

Despite the well-studied case of *Fortune*, the majority of states reject the application of the covenant to employment contracts. The covenant would, in essence, end employment-at-will and therefore, no good faith dealing for employees in those states!

If a worker is successful on a covenant of good faith and fair dealing claim, they may recover expectation damages (i.e., the lost benefits of the contract). The general goal is to return the injured employee to the position they would have been in without the breach of contract. This includes back pay and benefits minus anything the employee did or could have earned. Front pay may also be available. Front pay includes expected wages from the date of the judgment forward.

D. Tort Based Claims

Let's switch from Contracts class to Torts class. Although there could be a number of torts around the termination of employment, there are two which are the most common and available in most states.

1. Discharge in Violation of Public Policy

Most states recognize a cause of action for a termination against public policy. In fact, this was the first major modification of the at will rule back in the day and is very widely accepted. A principal justification for this public policy cause of action is that certain discharges that contravene established norms of public policy harm not only the specific employee but also the interests of the parties and society as a whole. Recognition of the public policy cause of action compels employers to internalize the costs of the harm they cause, and thereby encourages behavior consistent with those norms. That said, many states limit this claim to at-will employees. If an employee is working under a contract, they will need to proceed with a breach of contract claim. Further, some courts find that the public policy exception is not available if there is on-point statutory counterpart.

There are three elements to the claim:

1. The employee's conduct was protected by a public policy;
2. Dismissing the employee would undermine the public policy; and
3. Causal link between the conduct and the dismissal.

The first element is the source of much of the difficulty for employees. Employees need to identify the public policy which has been contravened.

A strict approach, adopted by some states, is that the public policy must be a fundamental and well defined public policy, found in a constitutional or statutory provision. Further, the policy must be clear. Some states allow administrative regulations to be a source of public policy because regulations are issued pursuant to statutory authority. A broader approach looks to judicial decisions as a source of public policy. An even broader approach will consider "the established interests of society," without a concrete source of law. Regardless of the source of the public policy, courts require the interest at issue to be a public interest, something that the termination of the employee would work against for the public at large and not just the individual worker.

Typically, actions by workers under this claim fall within four categories:

1. The worker refused to act in an unlawful manner;
2. The worker attempted to perform a required duty;
3. The worker exercised a right that the employee has;
4. The worker engaged in whistleblowing.[6]

Not every state tort law encompasses all four of these categories for its tort of wrongful discharge as against public policy but every state which recognized the tort includes at least one.

---

[6] Gantt v. Sentry Ins., 824 P.2d 680 (1992).

2. *Intentional Infliction of Emotional Distress ("IIED")*

We're still in Torts class. Keep in mind that in this context, we are considering the termination of employment. The elements for an IIED claim are:

- Extreme and outrageous conduct on the part of the employer;
- Intent to cause or disregard probability of causing severe emotional distress;
- A causal connection resulting in,
- Severe emotional distress.

Simply terminating an at will employee is not an IIED without something more. Typically, the something more generally falls on the manner of the termination. The manner of the termination must be truly outrageous, not simply a termination that's a shock to the worker. Courts will look to the context and relationship between the parties. The strict approach to this tort holds that certain levels of outrageousness in the workplace and criticism are part of the working life. A broader approach finds that an employer's abuse of power may contribute to a finding of outrageousness. Actions like using vile language, racial slurs, or fabricating evidence against an employee can contribute to a finding of outrageousness.

IN SUMMARY: The default of at-will employment, which provides no security of employment, has important exceptions. Public employees have constitutional protections and whistleblower statutes provide protections. Employees may not be at-will if they are working pursuant to a contract or a collective bargaining agreement. Employers may restrict themselves, either procedurally or substantively, through an employee handbook. The key restriction, either self-imposed or through statute or common law, is the requirement that the employer have "good cause." In addition, the state tort of wrongful discharge in violation of public policy, although not easy to show, gives employees another method to challenge terminations.

CHAPTER 10

Obligations of Employees

Employees have obligations to their employers during, and in some cases, after employment. These obligations may arise from contracts or from statutes. The overarching theme is that the employee has a duty to protect the employer's interest.

A. Contractual Obligations

1. *Express Terms*

Contractual obligations may arise from express or implied terms. Express terms typically include the duration of employment, the job responsibilities, the salary, and the amount of notice required to terminate employment. As you may recall from your Contracts class, there are conditions which excuse nonperformance of contracts and these may apply as well in employment contracts. One of the most common reasons is illness. However, if the illness is caused by the nonperforming party or the condition was foreseeable when contract was entered, then the nonperformance is not excused. Other conditions include:

- Incapacity
- Undue influence
- Duress
- Fraud
- Act of God (a tornado hits the plant and there isn't a workplace)
- Illegality
- Intoxication
- Misrepresentation

If an employee breaches the contract without a legally valid excuse, he will be liable for damages. Generally, the damages will encompass compensation for losses flowing from the breach. Think of the costs of hiring a new employee—the training, the search firm fees. The damages must be proven to a reasonable certainty and must be within the contemplation of the parties—your basic contract stuff!

2. *Implied Terms*

Just as there are implied duties on employers, there may be implied duties on employees. The most important of these is the **duty of loyalty**. Any employee considered an agent has a duty of loyalty to the principal. Basically, this duty requires the agent to refrain from competing with the principal—don't help competitors! Some courts only impose a duty of loyalty if the employee has a fiduciary relationship to the employer. (Typically, at-will employees do not have fiduciary relationships.)

Imagine the very common scenario of a current employee deciding to leave and start her own business. The implied duty of loyalty might be violated if that current employee contacts customers to solicit business or tries to lure away co-workers to the new venture. State law generally distinguishes between preparations to leave and active competition. It's the difference between "Just wanted you to know I'm leaving next week" and "I'm starting my own salon. You should come with me!" Courts look to the nature of the employment relationship, the impact of the employee's actions on the employer's operations, and the benefits promised to co-workers to jump ship. Courts disagree as to whether solicitation of at-will employees may be a breach of this duty of loyalty. If this duty is breached, the disloyal employee may be liable for the compensation they earned during the breach.

Also, anything that helps current competitors will be a violation of the implied duty of loyalty, especially if the employee is using the employer's resources to do so. This overlaps with the law surrounding trade secrets, discussed next.

B. Trade Secrets

As with much of employment law, this area is governed by state law (unless there is some conflict with federal patent law). However, most states have adopted the Uniform Trade Secrets Act ("UTSA").

The first question, of course, is what's a trade secret? The definition is broader than you might think. Not only might it be a plan, process, design, or formula but it could be an information collection (think of customer lists) that gives an advantage to the employer over competitors. It could also be the method of production of goods or a business function. Pricing information and marketing strategies have been held to be trade secrets. The key element is that it must be *secret* (shhhhh). Courts will look to see if the employer has taken steps to keep the information secret. For example, are there agreements with employees to keep the information secret? Is it encrypted somehow?

So, the formula for Coca-Cola is a trade secret but so might be the special process for those perfect highlights. General knowledge and skill an employee acquires during employment is not a trade secret; nor is anything commonly known in the industry.

Customer lists are often the subject of trade secret litigation. Courts ask how much effort went into creating the list and how easy it is to compile the list. If the list could be complied from the neighborhood directory, then the list isn't a trade secret. Basically, courts look to the time, effort, and expense put in to the list.

The relevant tort is **misappropriation of a trade secret**. There are two elements: 1) a trade secret; 2) was misappropriated. (Clever, right?). The second element is met when a trade secret was acquired and the person knows it was acquired improperly or there was disclosure of the trade secret by a person who acquired the trade secret improperly. This means that both the person disclosing the trade secret and the person receiving the trade secret may be subject to suit.

Now, how does this work for whistleblowers? As you might imagine, whistleblowers release confidential documents as part of their whistleblowing (otherwise, who will believe them?). Taking confidential information is a violation of the obligations to employers, of course, But courts will excuse this violation in the case of whistleblowing under a reasonableness standard. Was it reasonable under the circumstances to take employer's confidential documents? States all have their own tests for which circumstances met this reasonableness standard.

C. Noncompete Agreements

Sometimes called restrictive covenants, non-compete agreements try to keep former employees from working in the same industry for some period of time. According to the Federal Trade

Commission ("FTC"), 18% of workers in the US are covered by non-competes.[1] Until spring of 2024, state law governed in this area. Some states prohibited non-competes entirely, some prohibited them unless connected to the sale of a business. The FTC enacted a rule which prohibits most non-competes. Let's begin with the traditional tests and then discuss the new regulation from the FTC.

1. *Traditional Test*

As mentioned, some states prohibit non-competes entirely. In those states that don't, employees may be held to an enforceable non-compete. To be enforceable, the agreement must be designed to **protect a business interest, supported by consideration,** and **reasonable in scope.** A business interest could be a trade secret, confidential information, good will, or client relationships. The consideration to support a non-compete doesn't have to be separate consideration from the basic employment contract as long as there is consideration for that initial contract. But if the employer tries to add a noncompete during employment, then there must be additional consideration.

Lots of the fights about non-competes turn on the scope. The scope of a non-compete can contain a **geographic restriction**, a **time restriction,** and an **activity restriction.** Imagine a personal trainer at a gym. Is it reasonable for the non-compete to restrict the trainer from working as a personal trainer for five years anywhere in the state? Courts will consider whether the restriction is unduly difficult on the employee and this will turn on the scope of the employer's business and the nature of the employee's work. In considering the geographic area, the important factors are the area in which the employer competes and the area in which the employee works. For time restrictions, some states have statutory

---

[1] https://www.ftc.gov/news-events/news/press-releases/2024/04/ftc-announces-rule-banning-noncompetes.

time maximums (for example, one year). A non-compete can't be so arduous that it prevents the former employee from earning a living for too long. The reasonableness of these restrictions can turn on the specific industry.

If a non-compete is unreasonable, some states will enforce a noncompete that is too broad by narrowing the scope to render it a reasonable restriction. Other states will simply not enforce the non-compete. Finally, if the former employee was fired, this can be a factor in the enforceability of the non-compete. Whether the employee is fired for misconduct will be considered. Because it wouldn't be fair to fire an employee and then keep them from working at another job. On the other hand, if an employee purposefully engages in some bad behavior, gets fired, and then triumphantly goes off to the compete against the employer because the non-compete isn't enforceable, that would not be an optimum result!

2. Non-Competes: Are They over??

In April 2024, the Federal Trade Commission announced a new rule that finds non-compete clauses to be a method of unfair competition (and therefore banning such clauses).

As defined in the rule, a non-compete clause means:

> (1) A term or condition of employment that prohibits a worker from, penalizes a worker for, or functions to prevent a worker from:
>
> (i) seeking or accepting work in the United States with a different person where such work would begin after the conclusion of the employment that includes the term or condition; or

(ii) operating a business in the United States after the conclusion of the employment that includes the term or condition.[2]

Under this rule, existing non-competes are not enforceable. There is a small exception for existing non-competes for senior executives. Senior executives are defined as workers earning more than $151,164 annually and who are in policy-making positions. However, after the effective date of the rule, even executives will not be bound by new non-competes.

The FTC made clear that employers do not need to formally rescind all non-competes but such agreements are not enforceable. The FTC recommends that employers should use trade secret laws and non-disclosure agreements instead.

There is plenty of criticism of this new rule. First, the definition is such that it might apply to non-solicitation agreements if the agreement is too broad in its terms. Further, as of this writing, the rule has been challenged by the Chamber of Commerce arguing that FTC does not have authority to enact this rule. Stay tuned!

D. Inventions

Employees create many wonderful things while at work. The question is **who owns those inventions**? Many employers resolve this question through the employment contract, requiring employees to assign any inventions created during their employment to the employer. If there isn't a contractual agreement, the answer turns on **when and with what resources the employee created the invention**. If the worker is rightfully considered an employee and creates the invention during work time, with employer provided resources, the employer will a right to that invention. If the employee was hired to specifically create

[2] 89 Fed. Reg. 38342 (May 7, 2024).

the invention, then the employee has an obligation to assign the patent to the employer. If the employee wasn't hired to solve some problem but created something fabulous anyway, then the employer has a non-exclusive right to use the invention. This is known as the "shop right rule."

Finally, some states have enacted statutes that prevent employers from requiring employees to assign their inventions if doing so would be unfair or inequitable.

IN SUMMARY: Employees must met their contractual obligations, both express and implied. Further, employees have a duty to act in the best interest of the employer which usually boils down to not competing with the employer. (Don't bite the hand that feeds you.) Employees may also have an obligation to assign all inventions they help create to the employer but this will depend on the understanding of the parties and the resources used to create the invention. Post-employment, former employees have obligations to protect their former employer's trade secrets from disclosure. Many employees work under a non-compete agreement. However, if the new FTC rule withstands the challenges, these type of agreements will be unlawful.

CHAPTER 11

Post Employment Obligations by Employers

Believe it or not but employers have obligations to employees after the employment ends. In the next chapter, we'll discuss retirement and pension obligations but for now, let's consider two other topics: plant closings and unemployment benefits.[1]

A. Plant Closings

When an employer shuts down a plant or has a big layoff, this has an impact on not only the workers but the local community as well. Congress decided to get involved in 1988 with the Worker Adjustment and Retraining Notification Act ("WARN").[2] The WARN Act does not prevent a plant from closing but rather, as the name implies, requires that employers give notice of certain events.

Let's turn to the question you know you need to ask: **which** employers are covered by the Act? The Act covers a "business

[1] References for former employees is another area of post-employment obligations. Chapter Three discusses this.

[2] 29 U.S.C. §§ 2101-2109.

enterprise" with at least 100 employees. **What** is required? Employers must give sixty calendar days notice to the union if there is one, each worker if there is no union, and state and local officials. More specifically, the notice must be given to "affected employees" which means people who are reasonably expected to lose their jobs. **When** do employers need to give this notice? The 60 day notice needs to be provided when there is a plant closing or mass layoff. Plant closing means shutting down a single site that results in loss of work for at least 50 employees. A mass layoffs means employment loss at a single site of 33% of EEs at the site or more than 500 employees.

There are a few fairly big exceptions. If the employer can prove there was an "**unforeseen business circumstance**," then the 60 day provision is excused but notice must be given as soon as practicable. The employer has burden of proof that exception applies by proving that there were unforeseen circumstances and that the layoffs were caused by that circumstance. A second exception applies if the employer was trying to obtain new capital to save the plant or prevent the mass layoffs and wasn't successful. Further, the employer has to show that giving the 60 days notice would have reduced the chance of getting the capital. If all this is shown, then the employer is excused from the notice period. Although this may seem obvious, if the plant closes due to a natural disaster (a tornado destroys the plant), then the 60 day notice is simply not possible. Similarly, the Act is not applicable if the government makes the decision to shut down the plant. Employers may also offer a good faith defense of objective good faith.

If the employer doesn't provide the right notice? The WARN Act provides for fines of $500/day per day of violation and back pay for each day of violation for each aggrieved employee and costs. Enforcement is carried out by the aggrieved employees or local governments. Finally, the WARN Act is not an exclusive remedy, other state laws or contractual obligations governing shut downs may still apply.

B. Unemployment Benefits

1. *The Basics*

Unemployment insurance is a federal plan that is financed through a tax on payrolls.[3] Unemployment benefits cover employees only (not independent contractors). The federal insurance is the floor, states may go above this but not below. When an unemployed person files a claim seeking benefits, the state notifies the former employer to allow them to contest the claimant's eligibility. The employer might want to contest the eligibility because the annual unemployment insurance tax is substantially based on claims paid to that employer's former workers. In general, states are prohibited from providing benefits to undocumented workers not authorized to work. Benefits are typically provided for up to 26 weeks and is generally 50% of the worker's previous weekly wage.

The tricky part for a Short and Happy summary is that each state has its own unemployment system with its own eligibility requirements. There are two threshold eligibility requirements—the type of job and the amount of wages earned in the state. States set the amount of wages which must have be earned in a year in the state and often certain occupations are excluded from the eligibility for unemployment. For example, states exclude seasonal agricultural workers unless they have earned a minimum amount in some other occupation. Many states exclude domestic workers and student workers. These state rules for eligibility for unemployment benefits will be upheld as long as there is a rational basis for the rule.

---

[3] Federal Unemployment Compensation Act, 42 U.S.C. §§ 501-594, 1101-1105.

If the job category is covered and the employee has earned enough wages, there are three basic requirements:

1. separation must be involuntary;
2. you must be ready and able to work and;
3. you must accept suitable work.

2. *Involuntary Separation*

The standard rule is that you are not eligible for unemployment if you quit your job. Because if you quit, that means you are voluntarily unemployed. There is an important exception, however. An employee may still be eligible if it is a **"good cause quit"**. Some states require the good cause to be **attributable to the employer**, others do not.

a. Good Cause Quit

Good cause typically means a reason for rejecting work that would be deemed valid by reasonable men and women.[4] Attributable to the employer typically means a reason which is caused or created by the employer or is the result of actions by the employer. Usually there are requirements of reasonableness and good faith. Some examples of good cause include quitting when the employer **changes the job duties** (for example, a first grade teacher being transferred to a special education classroom) or quitting to move due to a significant other's job change. (Just remember—this is a state law determination). Resigning under **duress** would be considered an involuntary separation and therefore the employee would remain eligible for benefits. Some courts have found that the employer moving a far distance away and thus creating a difficult

[4] Labor disputes can raise some tricky issues. If an employee is unemployed because the union is on strike, he is disqualified for benefits. If the employer is engaged in a lockout of the employees, then it is more likely that the employee is entitled to benefits.

commute for the former employee is a reasonable reason to quit. Many courts have found that quitting due to a **hostile work environment** is a good cause to quit employment. Although a standard rule is that employees must take reasonable steps to preserve employment (i.e. try and fix any problems before quitting), this rule does not apply for sexual harassment cases. Resigning due to matters of **conscience** may also be considered a good cause quit. Or at least, an employee who resigns due to religious convictions will not be excluded from benefits because to deny benefits would be a First Amendment violation.

b. Misconduct

At this point, you may be saying to yourself, okay, as long as the employee is fired, she is entitled to unemployment benefits. Of course, it's not that easy! There is another exception. Employees fired due to misconduct are not eligible for unemployment compensation. There is a very important distinction between being fired for cause, as we discussed in Chapter 9, and being fired for misconduct. Misconduct is generally defined as the willful or wanton disregard of an employer's interest that is found in a deliberate violation or disregards of standards of behavior, carelessness, or negligence. Misconduct must be related to the job. A classic example in textbooks involves a medicar driver who managed to cause three collisions when diving in reverse. Three! There is certainly good cause to fire him but there is no misconduct because the driver was not deliberately violating a rule. Because unemployment benefits are supposed to be a safety net, courts generally do not find one instance of poor judgment as misconduct. Further, the employer rule that is violated must be a reasonable rule.

IN SUMMARY: Remember an employee may be fired for cause but that does not mean that there is misconduct that renders the employee ineligible for unemployment benefits.

3. Availability to Work

The next category of requirements for eligibility involves what is called availability to work. Sometimes this requirement is phrased as "willing, able, and ready to work." Here, courts look to the employee's ability to work, including whether the employee is qualified to perform the available jobs. Available also means, of course, that you are able to show up to the job. If the employee is a pharmacist and moves to a remote island in Michigan without a pharmacy, then that pharmacist is not available to work.

4. Suitable Work

Often disputes over unemployment benefits turn on whether the former employee is rejecting "suitable work." Employees must accept all suitable work in order to demonstrate that the former employee has a **good faith desire to be employed**. Courts look to whether there is good cause to refuse work. Good cause can be found if the job is not commensurate with the employee's skill level and pay. This is judged on a reasonableness standard in light of the circumstances in each case. States have different tests for deciding if the work is suitable. For example, Pennsylvania has a balancing test that will look to see how long the former employee has been out of work and balance it against the details of the offer of the new job. The longer you have been out of work, the less equal the state expects the job to be in order to be suitable. New York has held that there is not good cause to refuse employment when the fact that the salary offered is less than previously earned by the former employee. Refusing work deemed suitable will lead to a conclusion that the former employee is voluntarily unemployed and will not receive benefits.[5]

IN SUMMARY: Employers have obligations to provide notice if a large lay-off will occur. Employers' post-obligations are primarily in the area of unemployment benefits. Although the unemployment benefits do not come directly from the employer, because the employers insurance payment obligations are tied to the number of former employees seeking unemployment benefits, employers take care to make sure former employees are indeed eligible. Each state sets its own eligibility criteria for the amount of wages that must be earned in order to qualify. Employees must be involuntary unemployed unless they quit for a good cause (a legal term of art). Further, the employee must not have been fired for misconduct. To receive unemployment benefits, employees must continue seeking work and accept suitable employment offers.

[5] Federal statutes prohibits states from denying compensation for refusing work if the position offered is vacant due to a strike or if the job being offered would require the former employee to join a union or refrain from joining a union.

CHAPTER 12

Retirement

There are two overarching questions for retirement—when and with what benefits? Before we turn to the more complicated questions of pensions, let's consider the timing of retirement.

A. Mandatory Retirement

Most employees choose when to retire. In fact, the Age Discrimination in Employment Act prohibits mandatory retirement. (Remember, the ADEA only applies to employers with 20 or more employees.) There are a few exceptions to this prohibition. Bona fide executives or high level policy makers may be mandatorily retired at age 65. State and local governments may set mandatory retirement ages for law enforcement officers and firefighters. Sixty is a common mandatory age that states adopt. Finally, some federal regulations may set retirement ages for certain occupations. For example, commercial airline pilots must retire at age 65.

In addition, if an employer is able to prove the BFOQ defense allowed in the ADEA, then employees may be retired (or not hired). To refresh your memory, the BFOQ test requires an employer to prove that all or substantially all of the workers over a certain age would not be able to safely and efficiently perform the functions of the age AND that it is impracticable for the employer to test everyone on an individual basis.

Early retirement incentives are a tool that employers use to nudge employees out the door. There is no law that requires employers to provide such benefits but once they offer an early retirement incentive package, they must do so on a nondiscriminatory basis.

B. Pensions

Unlike many other areas of employment law, there is a federal statute on point. Remember ERISA from Chapter 6 when discussing healthcare? Well, she's back! In addition to healthcare plans, ERISA also applies to pensions. Remember that ERISA does not require employers to provide a pension plan but if they do choose to do so, then ERISA requires the plan to meet certain standards. ERISA uses tax incentives to encourage employers to offer pension benefits. Importantly, ERISA preempts most state laws in the area of employee benefits.

Let me be honest. ERISA is a very detailed statute that interacts with and involves the tax code. My Employment Law professor used to do a jazz hands wave while saying "ERISAAAAA" in a kind of mysterious voice.[1] If you decide to become an expert in ERISA, you will have a job for life. So we are not going to dive into the details but keep this Short and Happy. Let's consider the basic issues.

1. Who Is Covered?

Only employees are covered. Once again, this is helpfully defined as "any individual employed by an employer." Thanks,

---

[1] Shoutout to Professor Stewart Schwab.

ERISA. As discussed in Chapter Two, the Supreme Court in *Nationwide Mutual Insurance v. Darden* used the common law test of agency. The Court set forth several factors to consider in determining whether an individual is an employee and therefore protected by ERISA:

- the skill required
- who provided the tools necessary to complete the job
- the location of the work
- the duration of the relationship
- may the hiring party assign additional tasks to the worker
- may the hiring party determine the hours of the worker
- is the work part of the regular business of the hiring party
- provision of benefits.[2]

2. *What Counts as a Plan?*

First, the employer provided benefits have to qualify as a "plan" established or maintained by an employer for the protections of ERISA to kick in. The test most commonly cited is from the 11th Circuit in *Donovan v. Dillingham.*[3] The Court looked to four factors to decide whether the benefits program qualifies as a "plan" under ERISA:

1. Intended benefits;
2. Intended beneficiaries;

---

[2] Nationwide Mutual Insurance Co. v. Darden, 503 U.S. 318 (1992).

[3] 688 F.2d 1367 (11th Cir. 1982).

3. Source of financing;
4. Procedure to apply for and collect benefits.

Later, the Supreme Court added another factor—whether there is ongoing plan administration.[4] Certain plans are exempt from ERISA, including government pension plans, religious organization plans,[5] and plans to pay for other employee benefits (such as workers' compensation). One time payment programs (such as severance pay) are not considered "plans."

3. *What Does ERISA Require?*

There are requirements for how a plan is established (including a written document naming at least one plan trustee and stating how the plan may be amended). There are also reporting and disclosure requirements, including a summary plan description and an annual report.

4. *What Are the Plan Types?*

Plans generally come in two types: defined benefit and defined contribution. Under a defined benefit plan, the employer provides a fixed, pre-determined amount to the retired employee.[6] Often this is a monthly payment but can also be a lump sum. Under a defined contribution plan, the employer or the employee (or both) contributes a set amount to an individual employee's account and that amount is then invested. A 401(k) is probably the most common defined contribution plan.

Well, who cares what type of plan it is, you might say? ERISA cares! Because defined benefit plans promise employees a set

---

[4] Fort Halifax Packing Co. v. Coyne, 482 U.S. 1 (1987)

[5] These plans can include religiously affiliated businesses, such as hospitals. *See* Advocate Healthcare v. Stapleton, 581 U.S. 1652 (2017).

[6] There is also a cash balance plan. This is technically a defined benefit plan but defines the benefit as an account balance.

amount upon retirement, employer plans must meet funding requirements so that the funds are available upon retirement. However, under a defined contribution plan, once the employer makes the required contribution, it has met its obligations.

For both types of plan, ERISA provides for participation standards and vesting standards. Participation means the employee's ability to enroll in the plan. Employers may set the eligibility criteria as they like as long as it is based on a neutral business reason. However, eligible employees must be able to enroll once they are 21-years-old and have worked at the employer for one year.

ERISA's vesting provisions are the key protections of the statute. The vesting provisions are of primary importance to the defined benefit plans. There are two ways for employees to be vested. Under the first scheme, employees are fully vested after five years but not at all vested prior to that. Under the second method, employees become incrementally vested starting after two years with full vesting at seven years. Once the employee is fully vested, employees cannot lose the benefits even if they leave that place of employment. ERISA also creates termination insurance and establishes the Pension Benefit Guaranty Corporation to administer the program.

5. *Fiduciaries*

ERISA requires employers to designate one or more fiduciaries to administer the plan. As discussed in Chapter 6, ERISA creates fiduciary obligations for the people who administer the plan. A great deal of ERISA litigation focuses on whether an individual is a fiduciary or a non-fiduciary. Although there are statutory definitions for fiduciaries (and exceptions), designation as a fiduciary turns on the actual job duties performed. In general, employers are not fiduciaries unless they exercise some sort of discretionary authority over the benefit plan.

The duties of a fiduciary are designed to ensure that the fiduciary's actions are solely for the benefit of the plan and to act as a "prudent investor." So, a fiduciary has a duty of care and a duty of loyalty. Further, the Supreme Court has held that plan administrators have a duty to inform plan participants of relevant information over and above the reporting and disclosure requirements.[7]

6. *Claims*

If any of these obligations are violated, plan participants may sue and bring claims to recover benefits, enforce rights, and for breach of fiduciary duty. There is also a catch all provision which allows participants to sue for equitable relief. In determining whether ERISA has been violated, the standard of review at issue will turn on the amount of discretion the plan places with the plan administrator. The decision is reviewed under a *de novo* standard unless the plan gives the administrator or fiduciary discretion to determine eligibility for benefits or to construe the terms of the plan. If there is discretion, then courts review under the abuse of discretion standard. The abuse of discretion standard is a much more lenient standard for the plan and therefore, a more difficult standard for the beneficiary to prove a violation. As you can imagine, there is LOTS of caselaw concerning whether the administrator has discretion. In the end, most plans include "magic words" providing the administrator with final decision making in denial or approval of benefits. It is this final decision making authority that creates the discretion and thus earns the more lenient review standard for any decisions under the plan.

---

[7] Varity Corp. v. Howe, 516 U.S. 489 (1996).

Finally, employers are prohibited from retaliating against anyone who exercises a right under a benefit plan (such as firing someone before vesting in order to prevent having to pay the pension).

C. A Note on Social Security Benefits

The Social Security system provides Old Age and Survivor Benefits. When former employees receive these benefits, of course, the payments are coming from the government and not from the employer directly. The employer's obligations end when the employer has deducted the requisite amount from each paycheck.

That said, it is an important source of income for retired employees and eligibility for these benefits is dependent on spending a set amount of time in the workforce. There are three basic eligibility requirements. First, the appropriate tax credits for working the statutory amount. Second, reaching the age of 62 for partial credits and age 65 for full benefits. However, this full benefit age has been raised to 67 for anyone born after 1960. (I know, I know, will there even be Social Security benefits when you, Dear Reader, retire?) The final eligibility requirement is that the retired employee must have applied for the benefits!

> **IN SUMMARY:** Unless the employer falls within one of the exceptions under the ADEA, the employer cannot compel employees to retire. They may (but are not required to) offer early retirement incentives. Employers again may (but are not required to) offer pension benefits. Once an employer choose to have pension benefit plan, the plan must meet the requirements of ERISA, the most important involving the vesting of employees' benefits and the duties of the plan administrators. Administrators must act as prudent investors and with a duty of loyalty to the plan participants.

CHAPTER 13

Arbitration

Arbitration is a form of dispute resolution that is less formal than litigation because the dispute is decided by an impartial arbitrator rather than a judge and it takes place in an office rather than a court room. In an arbitration hearing, parties present evidence and the arbitrator may ask questions of the parties and their witnesses. Further, the rules of evidence, discovery, and motion practice are all relaxed. Ultimately, the arbitrator makes a decision that is final, in writing, and binding.

Why spend any time talking about arbitration in a book about Employment Law? Because, by many estimates, at least 60 million employees work under a clause that compels them to take any employment disputes to binding arbitration. Most of these employees did not negotiate for the arbitration clause. Instead, the clause was simply part of the employment agreement or in the employment handbook. Employers (and employees) favor arbitration because it is quicker and cheaper than litigation. However, many employees feel arbitration is skewed in favor of employers because of lack of transparency, restrictions on collective actions, and potential bias. And keep in mind that a clause requiring binding arbitration means that employees lose the ability to go to court to resolve an employment dispute, limiting their legal recourse and rights.

Because arbitration is a private agreement between employers and employees, typically there hasn't been a fight over the arbitration of contractual rights. In fact, requiring arbitration is common in many collective bargaining agreements. The real fight turns on compelling arbitration of statutory rights (such as discrimination claims).

The background legislation for this area is the Federal Arbitration Act ("FAA") of 1925[1] which embodies a strong policy in favor of arbitration. If the FAA had a vibe, it would be "we love arbitration!" For years, there was some confusion as to whether the FAA applied in the employment context because there is an exception in the statute for certain workers. Specifically, Section 1 states "nothing herein contained shall apply to contracts of employment of seamen, railroad employees, or any other class of workers engaged in foreign or interstate commerce." Hmmm, what does this mean? Well, the Supreme Court has some thoughts.

A. Arbitration in Employment Disputes

In the early days, courts didn't enforce arbitration clauses if the right at issue was a statutory right (again, think of a race discrimination claim). The Court first applied the FAA to employment cases in 1991 in *Gilmer v. Interstate/Johnson Lane Corp.*, 500 U.S. 20, 33 (1991). There, the plaintiff brought an age discrimination claim, but there was an arbitration clause in his registration with the Stock Exchange. The Court held that pre-dispute arbitration agreements between employee and employer are enforceable even if statutory (as opposed to contractual) rights are at issue. The only way the Court would refuse to enforce the

---

[1] 9 U.S.C. §§ 1-16.

arbitration clause is if the source for the claim (here, the ADEA) barred arbitration.

Gilmer didn't involve an employment contract, however. The Court reached that issue in *Circuit City Stores, Inc. v. Adams*, 532 U.S. 105 (2001). In this case, the Court interpreted the "contracts of employment" language quoted above. It held that this exception only applied to people working in interstate transportation. Although this may seem like a nice, straightforward answer, it didn't completely resolve all of the questions. You can imagine there are questions of what counts as working in Interstate transportation or being a "transportation worker." Does a taxi driver who takes someone from Manhattan to New Jersey count as an interstate transportation worker? Courts are still sorting through these issues.

After *Gilmer* then, it was clear that employers could make use of pre-dispute arbitration clauses for all non-interstate transportation workers. However, employees may still file administrative claims and agencies such as the EEOC may pursue discrimination claims against an employer even if there is an arbitration agreement with the specific employee.[2]

The Supreme Court is fully on the "we love arbitration" bandwagon, issuing numerous opinions over the last twenty years upholding arbitration clauses in employment agreements, whether collective or individual. In terms of collective action, the Court has upheld an arbitration clause in a collective bargaining agreement where the agreement waived rights to litigate statutory discrimination claims, provided that the waiver was "clear and unmistakable."[3] The Court has also allowed for arbitration agreements to prohibit class wide actions, finding that such clauses are not inherently unconscionable. Although lower courts refused to enforce uneven arbitration agreements, recent Supreme Court

---

2 EEOC v. Waffle House, Inc., 534 U.S. 279 (2002).

3 Wright v. Universal Maritime Service Cor., 525 U.S. 70 (1988).

decisions have called into question whether there is a basis to do so.

B. Defenses to Arbitration Clauses

Again, because arbitration is considered a private agreement between the employer and the employee, standard contract defenses may be raised. Typically, these questions arise in the formation of the agreement. Thus, if there was pressure to sign the arbitration agreement, not enough notice of the arbitration agreement, or modifications of the agreement without consideration, courts may decide to strike down the arbitration agreement. An argument of unequal bargaining power hasn't been a winning argument in the past. However, if a specific arbitration clause creates a process that is so restrictive that it prevents the vindication of the employee's rights, courts may refuse to enforce. This could come in the form of severely reduced remedies or restrictive presentation of evidence, for example. Finally, unconscionability has been raised on both procedural and substantive grounds. However, there is a presumption in favor of arbitration, including allowing the arbitrator to determine questions of enforceability!

C. Recent Developments

Recent developments in this area of law have focused on the interaction between litigation and arbitration and the preemption of state law by the FAA.

In 2022, Congress passed a law amending the FAA to prohibit employers from unilaterally enforcing arbitration agreements for claims of sexual assault or sexual harassment. The statute is named the Ending Forced Arbitration of Sexual Assault and Sexual Harassment Act.[4]

Recently, the Supreme Court has decided two cases centering on the trial courts' obligation to stay cases related to arbitration. First, in *Coinbase v. Suski*, the Court held that if a trial court finds an arbitration agreement unenforceable, it should stay the court proceedings while the decision is appealed.[5] Second, in *Smith v. Spizzirri*, a group of workers claimed that they were misclassified as independent contractors.[6] They sued in court for minimum wage payments and other benefits despite an arbitration agreement with the companies that used their services. The Court held that a trial court shouldn't dismiss a case simply because it was subject to arbitration. Rather the trial court should stay the proceedings while arbitration continues.

Finally, the Supreme Court found that the FAA preempted a California state law which prohibited arbitration of employment claims brought under the California Private Attorney General Act ("PAGA").[7] The Ninth Circuit reached a similar decision, finding that the FAA preempted California's law criminalizing the use of mandatory employee arbitration agreements.[8]

> **IN SUMMARY:** Unions may negotiate collective bargaining agreements that require all claims to be submitted to arbitration. Employers may require arbitration for individual employees, including statutory claims. An arbitration clause might be thrown out for standard contract defenses (but unlikely because "we love

4 H.R. 4445 (2022).
5 144 S.Ct. 1186 (2024).
6 144 S.Ct. 1173 (2024).
7 Viking River Cruises, Inc. v. Moriana, 143 S.Ct. 60 (2022).
8 Chamber of Com. v. Bonta, 2023 WL 5284806 (E.D. Cal. Aug. 16, 2023).

arbitration!”). And no arbitration is allowed for claims of sexual harassment or sexual assault.